Bare Hand Knitting

Tool-Free Knitting at Its Finest

Volume I

Bare Hand Knitting

Tool-Free Knitting at Its Finest

Volume I

by

Aleshanee Akin

Illustrations by Elizabeth Auer

Printed with support from the Waldorf Curriculum Fund

Published by:
Waldorf Publications at the
Research Institute for Waldorf Education
351 Fairview Avenue, Suite 625
Hudson, NY 12534

Title: *Bare Hand Knitting: Tool-Free Knitting at Its Finest*
   Volume I
Author: Aleshanee Akin
Illustrator: Elizabeth Auer
Copy editor: Patrice O'Neill Maynard
Proofreader: Ruth Reigel
Layout: Ann Erwin

Dedication

This book is dedicated to my beloved grandmother, Virginia Harvey Mathias. She had not thought herself skilled at handwork until, at age ninety-nine, she was happily surprised to discover she could knit a scarf with her bare hands. She always encouraged the creative spirit in her children and grandchildren and appreciated what made each one of us into unique individuals.

This book is also dedicated to all the children who will be shaping a better future with their bare hands.

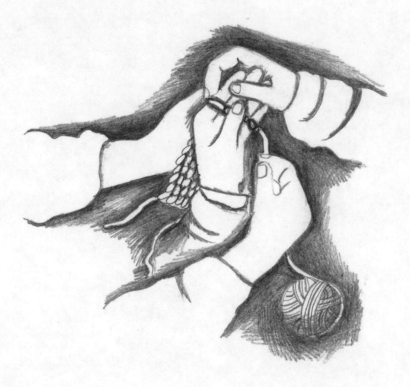

Table of Contents

Introduction
A Story of Healing

I introduce here a new and developing art that I call Bare Hand Knitting. This handcraft begins as simple finger knitting, but expands to utilize all ten fingers and countless variations of stitches and patterns. Some of the basic techniques, which I describe here, are fairly widely known. Others, I have invented—or, quite likely, re-invented, as they may well have been discovered at other times lost in the mists of pre-history. In vain I have searched for the origins of this craft but, indeed, without tools or an artifact such as the tiny bronze figurine what evidence could exist?

> So far we have no known representations of looms or weaving before the late Neolithic period … although we have narrow textiles quite early.[1]

E.J.W. Barber goes on to describe "a bronze figurine from Yunnan China from the Early Han Dynasty (late first millennium BC) of a "woman weaving on a backstrap loom with tension controlled by the toes."

As our ancient ancestors developed handcrafts to meet the practical needs of everyday life, they designed various tools for greater efficiency and uniformity. More elaborate devices followed. Today, anyone who wants a sweater or scarf or socks, never needs to pick up a pair of knitting needles—giant machines somewhere turn out these articles en masse. And yet, people still spin, weave, sew, and knit for the personal satisfaction such acts of creation bring. I have found that gratification is greatest when there is no extraneous tool between myself and the work—to have my fingers simply move within the wool and bring forth amazing creations feels like an act of profound magic.

Bare Hand Knitting is the art of transforming natural fibers and yarns into practical garments, accessories, or works of art, through a linked-stitch process. Barehand felting, beading, finger-knitting, and macramé are what I am referring to when I use the term *barehand crafts*.

It is appropriate that Bare Hand Knitting and crafts should emerge at this time. Cultural pockets of the modern world are eagerly returning to the fiber arts and other traditional handcrafts. There is a renewed interest in handmade items for their quality and aesthetic value. The therapeutic benefits of working with the hands are, now more than ever, being recognized. There is a growing movement away from dependency on large and foreign sources of goods for our everyday needs and toward an increase in independent and local community-based economies.

So how did this craft find its way into my life, personally? As an eleven-year-old child I discovered for myself an interesting method for knitting on the five fingers of one hand. I showed the technique to my crafts teacher, and I remember filling an entire summer with the happy exploration of this new kind of play.

Twenty years later I was intrigued to find the children in a small Waldorf school in Russia, where I was then teaching, engaging in a similar method.

Many more years went by. I was now living in New England with my three children, while completing my master's degree in education. I had all but forgotten my childhood yarn-play, when a nearly devastating crisis brought it back into my life. My oldest daughter, Daniella, who had been wearing a plastic retainer, developed a strong autoimmune response as a result of prolonged exposure to the plasticizers. The powerful allergic reaction caused her lips to repeatedly swell and peel, and also began to affect her mental stability. Even after we identified the problem and got rid of the retainer, she had become sensitized to many types of plastics. Even a sandwich from the cafeteria wrapped in plastic film would set her off. After an incident at school, she was placed in a mental hospital, from which, it turned out, it was difficult to have her released. We were demoralized by the treatment that she received. My institutionalized daughter was offered little in the way of recreation, but only the opportunity to view a television or pace a small hallway. She was continually drugged. She was not allowed outside for over a year.

I brought her knitting needles and yarn, and a staffer reported to me that my daughter spent many quiet, happy hours working on a colorful scarf. Then, while I was on an 80-mile walk for Mental Health Awareness, I received a sad call from Daniella telling me that all the knitting needles of the patients had been confiscated— there was an administrative decision that they might be unsafe.

It felt to us as though the very last, good thing had been taken from her. She was so sad, so helpless. It was only faith that kept us going; good friends and family that held us together. That is when my childhood barehand method came to mind. During our visits, I showed her some of the stitches I remembered, and she resumed knitting without the needles. At home, I began to develop new techniques, and during our visits I would share them with her.

Using the thick, soft, and colorful wool yarns that I brought to her (many of the skeins were donated by friends and by members of our church community) Daniella began to create beautiful and useful knitted pieces. This proved to be the turning point in her healing process,and brought my own life new meaning.

I continued to explore the possibilities throughout my ongoing winter visits with my daughter. We rolled balls of yarn and shared new discoveries with each other. The work she did with her hands was not only beautiful; it had a therapeutic effect on her. She created scarves, hair-pieces, and wet-felted wool jewelry. I created dolls, mermaids, and hats. The most amazing thing is, we were having fun! A sense of joy returned to us, and we both began to feel hope again—as if we had retaken the threads of our destinies back into our own hands.

My daughter's beautiful scarves were soon being worn by family and friends. A sense of connection to the world outside helped Daniella to rebuild her self-esteem and to connect with folks back home, even during her isolation.

I believe that the integrative aspect of Bare Hand Knitting also worked as an effective treatment for her. Studies show that activities that require both hemispheres of the brain to work together have a therapeutic effect in cases of phobia and PTSD. A well-accepted therapy called EMDR, involves focusing the eyes on a moving image that passes from side-to-side across the midline, or listening with earphones to sounds that go from one ear to the other, or a vibration passing from one hand to the other, in order to integrate both hemispheres of the brain while simultaneously bringing up traumatic memories.[2]

It is not unreasonable to suggest that more engaging midline-crossing activity shouldn't work as well or better. Japanese researcher, Ryuta Kawashima, has shown that the thoughtful and creative activity of finger-knitting lights up far more areas of the brain than does the mindless act of twiddling the fingers. Furthermore, the methods that were used in his study, which give such remarkable results, were the most basic of bare-hand techniques found in the first part of this book.

And, as far as child development goes, researchers have repeatedly shown that handwork stimulates intelligence and cognitive development.[3]

The beautiful colors and soft natural fibers offered the only alternative to the cold, harsh, and stale surroundings of my daughter's unit. She shared her donated yarn with other patients in her ward and began teaching them, and even some of the staffers, how to knit with their bare hands. Soon, during my visits, I saw new smiles on what had previously been some very morose faces. I remember one older, long-term patient beaming with pride as she showed me the scarf she had just made.

After a lot of Bare Hand Knitting, as well as prayer, by springtime, my daughter had made enough progress to defy the pessimistic expectation of her psychiatrist. She now has a normal life in California, attending our local community college and getting good grades.

This book is your entry into what I hope you will find to be a very pleasant recreational art form. While the use of extraneous tools is an important aspect of being human, our own hands are the most amazing tools we have. It is also my hope that this craft will reach many of those who are closed off in mental hospitals and prisons, where they may not have access to pointed knitting needles and who, as a result, have not been able to benefit from the therapeutic effects of fiber-handwork.

Young children traditionally enjoy playing countless hand movement games, and for good reason. I trained and worked as a Waldorf teacher, and Waldorf educators look to hand and finger play as an important aspect of the curriculum in Early Childhood and beyond and as a tool for awakening the various capacities of the mind. More challenging finger activities such as cat's-cradle and large-needle knitting are taught to first-graders. Such activities have been found to facilitate literacy. Gross-motor and fine-motor movements of varying types and degrees are important for overall learning and healthy

development. Specific movement patterns are known to be therapeutic and integrative.[4,5,7]

In Hindu tradition, the stimulation of various mudra points on our fingers is believed to be healing, and recent studies have lent support to these claims.[6] Many of the barehand methods seem to invoke hand-yoga, and who knows what mystical connection might lie therein.

I find it truly amazing that in practical application, virtually anything that can be created by knitting and crocheting can also be made by the bare hands alone. (Even a custom-fitted five-fingered glove!) And new barehand methods, patterns, and techniques—such as cooperative knitting-circles, combined wet-felting/barehand techniques, and combined-macramé—continue to develop through my work.

While this book is primarily aimed at a general audience, as an experienced teacher with a Master's Degree in Education from Antioch University, I have taken special care to consider the pedagogical aspect of each stitch and pattern I introduce. Certain tasks and movements are appropriate for specific stages of childhood development, and so I have provided a Curriculum section at the beginning of the book that includes my age recommendations.

For the last fifteen years, both before and after obtaining my degree, I have taught art and other special subjects in Waldorf schools in the US and Russia, as well as being a main-lesson teacher. For the past six years I have included instruction in barehand techniques, when and where it was helpful and appropriate. I am very encouraged with what I have seen. The rich and broad handwork curriculum already in place in Waldorf schools provides the students with important life skills. This creates a foundation for my work in barehand methods. Certain barehand techniques are also helpful in preparing children for traditional handwork skill sets. I see this form of handwork as a complement to all of the other valuable crafts that are so important in the development of the child, supporting their growth as capable, confident, and whole individuals.

At the end of each chapter you will find a vocabulary review for the new terms you will need to know. You will find it helpful to become familiar with the new words introduced in each chapter before going to the next.

The hands and minds of new practitioners must be given time to increase in dexterity and flexibility. Using this book, you will have the best results by moving through it chapter-by-chapter to build upon a new lexicon and skill set. This is a process that cannot be rushed. Be patient with yourself. Barehand crafts, just as any other worthwhile skill, cannot be learned overnight. It may help you to consider that it has taken me many years to progress to the point where I am now. There is much that I am able to accomplish quite easily now, that would have been impossible for me just one year ago. And I continue in exploring uncharted territory and improving my skills.

What I find beautiful in a barehand piece, I attribute not only to the intricate pattern of the stitching, but to the care and focus that went into it. There is an intention that calls to the spirit in this art form. The natural look and feel of it brings us back to ancient earth-friendly and people-loving fiber arts. The use of minimally processed and nontoxic fibers, dyes, and beads plays an important role in this.

Developing skills for making things with her own hands was emancipating for my daughter, and it is for me as well. Our culture, as a whole, has become so nervous, jangly, computer-driven, and tech-dependent. Bare Hand Knitting is, for me, the anti-tech antidote. It is like taking a vacation from the modern world. I wear an obsidian arrowhead necklace piece when I knit as a useful cutting implement that honors my ancestral roots and the non-consumer foundations of this art.

ENDNOTES

1. Barber, E.J.W. *Prehistoric Textiles: The Development of Cloth in the Neolithic and Bronze Ages with Special Reference to the Aegean.* Princeton, NJ: Princeton UP, 1991. Print, page 81.

2. EMDR Institute, "What Is EMDR?" "Eye Movement Desensitization and Reprocessing Therapy," *What Is EMDR Comments.* N.p., n.d. Web. 09 Jan. 2017.

3. Wilson, Frank R. *The Hand: How Its Use Shapes the Brain, Language, and Human Culture.* New York: Pantheon, 1998. Print.

4. Hess, Lory Widmer. "Spinning Straw into Gold: The Healing Potential Of Handwork" *Lilipoh* 16.62 (2011): 60-60. Consumer Health Complete – EBSCOhost. Web. 2 August 2014. (with reference to the following text in her Foreword): "Technical movements such as typing, are an intellectual construct that does not have the same effect. One of our course participants remarked that through spinning she could start to 'feel the brain' in a new way, having done clerical work with her hands in the past."

5. Weigle, M. *Spiders & Spinsters: Women and Mythology.* Albuquerque: University of New Mexico Press. 1982. "An account from a contemporary folklorist visiting a Navajo family. In reference to his question as to the origins of cat's cradle, or 'nettles shields' as they were called by the Native people.

   "During this conversation the mother has gone back to weaving momentarily and the other children are still doing string fingers. 'The spider woman taught us all these designs as a way of helping us to think. You learn to think when you make these.' 'And she taught us about weaving too,' a teenage girl puts in. 'If you can think well,' the first boy adds, 'you won't get into trouble or get lost. Anyway, that's what our father says.'"

6. Menen, Rajendar. *The Healing Power of Mudras: The Yoga of the Hands.* London: Singing Dragon, 2010. Print.

7. "Enduring Legacies Native Case Studies." Enduring Legacies Native Cases: N.p., n.d. Web, 12 January 2017.

chapter one

Barehand
Handwork Curriculum
Year by Year

Overview of Child Development

Handwork for the First Seven Years

Handwork enhances the mind of the developing child, and its rhythmic movements are calming to the nerves. With the emergence of so many children with special needs in classrooms today, how timely it is to bring in more fiber arts. We need very little to get started along this path. Just some natural fibers and our own two hands.

The entirety of what is taught in school has to do with the straight and the curved line and a relationship between the two. Handwork has traditionally been a child-friendly activity as it was practiced for millennia in its various forms within the home. With children present to observe and imitate them, parents and caregivers have gone busily about their daily tasks to provide food, shelter, and clothing. Spinning, weaving, felting, and knitting can also be summed up as manipulations of the straight line and a curved line. Our capacity for language and thought bear a relationship to the very movements that we make with our bodies and hands.

There is purpose behind these movements. Even today, handwork is practical for life. To follow this thread of logic, not only does handwork produce fabric, clothing, and shelter, but also the undertaking of a project creates pathways for human intelligence. There is also a social element to the fiber arts. Just as the warmth from the fire has helped make human connections by drawing people together and seeding civilizations with the fruits of cultural enrichment, traditional handwork techniques have required people to work together for efficiency to achieve the best results. Even the simple activity of rolling a ball of yarn from a hank, is carried out, most efficiently, between two people. The art of cloth-making has consumed an enormous portion of humanity's waking time, until very recently.

Looking to their caregivers, as well as at their peers, young children learn by imitating what goes on around them. The developing mind of the young child is intrinsically linked to the physical activity of the body and is informed by all of the senses.

Young children learn naturally in a warm, safe, and welcoming space that supports the daily rhythm of a well-functioning home life. Just as it is important to provide basic healthy foods to nourish a young body, an optimal educational program will also incorporate a vast array of opportunities for movements.

Engaging in indoor and outdoor free play is an important part of childhood. Activities such as circle games and nature walks involve large-motor movements. Stepping along a log, swinging, or riding a seesaw, develop balance. Activities such as folding napkins, picking berries, and engaging in handwork of all kinds involve fine motor movements and develop hand-eye coordination. Setting a regular time each day for growing children to rest is necessary. When children in their first seven years of life are in our care, and we, the parents or educators, engage in meaningful work, we provide for them the greatest lesson of all.

It is sad, indeed is a tragedy, that so much of what young people do and see today involves interfacing with a cold and lifeless screen. Screens, no matter what is on them, give us a flattened and deadened version of reality and do not develop the young mind. The power is within our hands to turn this around. As we, the adults, find our way back to meaningful work, the inner artisan can once again be reawakened for the generations to follow.

During those formative years, balance connects to our ability to hear, movement informs the development of speech recognition, warmth enlivens our interest in the world around us, and touch awakens our sense of self.

In the Waldorf early childhood classroom, children take part in cooking, cleaning, gardening, song, and dance. Meal preparation, basic household chores, and traditional artisans' crafts make up the foundation stones for the curriculum and are built into the natural flow of each day's routine. This means that, as teachers, we ourselves are practicing these skills with the children—we cook, we clean, we garden, and we engage in handcrafts. We tell stories; we create puppet shows; we are social. We strive to surround ourselves with beauty and leave room for the imagination in the children's objects for play. This rich curriculum provides the children with something worthy of imitation. All of this strengthens the very fabric of our beings.

When my youngest daughter Abby entered first grade, she already knew how to knit on large needles, which surprised both her teacher and me, because no one had actually taught her how to knit and she had never picked up knitting needles before. When asked how she was able to knit, she simply said that her kindergarten teacher, Miss Lisa, knitted, and that she liked to watch her. I shared this with Miss Lisa, who remembered that Abby had often sat by her side during outdoor free-play time as she, her teacher, knitted. But even Lisa had not realized that Abby had so carefully observed her in her technique. To this day, Abby enjoys all sorts of handcrafts.

This educational model reminds of us of what once existed as folk wisdom. It is a mistake to push book learning and abstractions on children too early— as is done in the majority of kindergartens today, where, a misguided effort to jump-start academic learning is deeply entrenched.

All activities for this age group can better be seen as a precursor to academic learning. A strong will and a sense of truth, beauty, and goodness are needed for sorting through the challenges that lay ahead—for the academics as well as for life itself. The significance of what we bring and the mood in which they are carried out is part of the teacher training.

A Complement to a Full Handwork Curriculum

Bare Hand Knitting is for everyone. The techniques in this book are fun for children and adults alike. I encourage you to learn and teach them freely, bringing your own inspirations into the mix. The classroom is another wonderful place to do handwork. It is very much encouraged that teachers of a variety of subjects consider integrating some barehand crafting into the lesson.

Opportunities to weave in related lessons in math, geometry, and art are very much present. Some examples for this will be pointed out along the way. Furthermore, students of all ages might enjoy having a project involving a simple activity, such

as finger knitting or yarn winding, close at hand while in school. Engaging in simple handwork stimulates the vestibular system and has been shown to have positive effects. This calming activity also heightens the ability to listen. As a result of this phenomenon, simple activities such as modeling with beeswax or finger-knitting are sometimes used to enhance focus and memory-retention during story-time or spoken lessons.

As early childhood and elementary school teaching has been such a focus in my life, some recommendations have been laid out below for parents, homeschool instructors, and teachers, who carry the responsibility for bringing in lessons at the age-appropriate level.

Age Recommendations

The barehand curriculum has been designed as a complement to a full handwork curriculum as an enrichment to, rather than a replacement for, traditional crafting skills. In certain special situations, barehand methods may be helpful as a preparation for a tool-based method.

There is a lot to take into consideration when assigning an appropriate age level to a given handwork skill. Below, recommendations are given for a child-development-sensitive approach. In general, Volume I deals with introductory level techniques, geared mainly toward the first nine years of life and beyond, to build a foundation for intermediate and advanced barehand techniques to be found in Volume II. Within each category,

there is some degree of flexibility for these age recommendations, depending on the level of support that is provided by a teacher or parent. However, for the most part, the intermediate and advanced techniques found in Volume II should not be taught directly to this young age group. The micro-movements required become increasingly complex for the young developing mind. Dominance is often still being sorted out in younger children. That being said, there is much still to be learned and researched on the barehand crafting front and, as these methods become more widely used, more will be learned from classroom observation.

Our brain treats the tools that we use like an extension of our own body. So, from this perspective, it makes sense to introduce handwork techniques with barehand methods.

Barehand Handwork Curriculum Year by Year

Birth to Age 6

Children should not be expected to produce a utilitarian "product" at this tender age. By modeling meaningful and life-sustaining work such as gardening, crafting, washing, harvesting, and food preparation, we give young children a wealth of activities to imitate. Their imitative play will also require access to earth and sand, wool and water, pots and pans and dough, and the like.

When it comes to handwork, the availability of a variety of natural materials helps to develop the sense of touch and the sense of life.

During the fifth year, a gradual transition can begin from pure play to process-oriented crafting. Early Childhood teachers have had success with this age group in a variety of basic crafting projects such as rolling of a ball of yarn (chapter 2), finger-knitting (chapter 4), and wet-felting balls (chapter 8).

Age 6

By the age of six, children are likely more than ready for the introduction of *Basic Hand Knitting* (also sometime called *Hand-Weaving*) (chapter 5), which is a nice way to ease them into the very useful and also pro-literacy activity of large-needle knitting.

In first- and second-grade handwork classes, vast amounts of small, logistical knitting problems do arise and must be worked through, in order for the projects to proceed. Research has established that knitting teaches logic in part through this problem-solving activity.

Basic Hand Knitting, although it carries a logic of its own, also requires hand-eye coordination and sequencing, both of which prepare the developing child for the activity of reading. Bulky yarns are preferable, as fine-motor skills are still developing. Tactile development and a sense of beauty and esthetics are best served by the use of natural fibers and colors derived from plant dyes.

Age 7

You will find that this age group is capable of taking on slightly more involved handwork projects. When it comes to traditional large-needle knitting, with help and encouragement, children of this age can already follow well-thought-out and clearly defined patterns. It should be expected that projects be brought to a point of completion by children by this age.

Projects involving the alternation of *chain* and *knit* (chapter 6) can be done at this age. Second-graders become very excited when there is a rich choice of colors to work with and are more likely to be self-motivated to see a project through to the end. The materials should still be soft, preferably on the thicker side, and natural.

Age 8

In general, eight-year-olds are lively and fun to work with. Begin with some basic projects that require *barehand whip-stitching* (chapter 7). Some more-complex *wet-felting* projects (chapter 8) can be undertaken in small groups and with support.

Looking Ahead

Figuratively speaking, nine-year-olds are at a point of stepping out of the almost magical dream-like consciousness of early childhood. Possibly one of the best ways we can offer them a sense of security is to give them some basic tools and fundamental skills for life. There are many useful and meaningful crafts that can be taught to this very able age group. Among these are lessons in the basics of fiber arts.

Basic handwork skills such as spinning, weaving, and plant-dying can make up an important part of a developmentally appropriate and childhood-enhancing curriculum for third graders. The concept of "sheep to shawl" is perfect for this age.

New Terms

In order to bring you this written instructional guide for Bare Hand Knitting, it was necessary to create a new lexicon. The new terms relate to the many, yet unfamiliar, micro-movements we will be doing with our fingers. Wherever possible, established knitting terminology has been adopted. Both the sequence-stories and the new vocabulary developed quite naturally from the intrinsic connections between images from nature and the form and movements of the human hand. (It sometimes seems to me, when describing hand movements in terms of nature, I am only responding to the handprints of our Creator.) Some barehand terms are introduced in chapter 2, and others appear throughout the book. A full glossary of terms is laid out at the end of each.

Once a technique has been introduced, it is broken down into the bare-bones steps that are listed in abbreviated form in the chapter review. The introduction of techniques is chronological, and you will want to be familiar with the terms of one chapter before moving along to the next.

In addition to the abbreviated breakdown for each technique, there is a visual component. Here, the illustrated version of the steps is mapped out in a very simplified reminder code. This code is used in place of the illustrated step-by-step instructions whenever a previously introduced concept occurs. In other words, each step is broken down and explained in detail only one time. After that, you must rely on the reminder codes which become the building blocks for learning new techniques. This system will continue for advanced techniques in Volume II.

Stitch Stories

You will notice that each foundational Bare Hand Knitting technique is introduced here along with a story or rhyme. Using stories and verses to pass along cultural information has been practiced since ancient times. Many progressive educators have re-introduced this learning tool for teaching children today. Adults can also benefit from these memory-aids when learning new techniques.

For teachers, bringing in a stitch story as preparation for a new handwork technique helps the lesson to go along fluidly and helps the children to remember the steps. The little sequence-stories shared in this book have been developed through my own teaching experience. Inspired by the stories told by Waldorf handwork teachers over the years, I have created little tales drawn from nature that fit with the micro-movements required of the fingers and hands for each method. You may use these or come up with your own.

If you have the chance to work with a group of children in advance of the handwork lesson, it works nicely to begin on the day prior by telling the story or rhyme for the following day's lesson. The next day, have the students retell the story. This would be a good moment to introduce a shortened version or rhyme if there is one, in conjunction with a demonstration of the finger gestures for the technique being learned.

Do not hesitate to repeat the story while showing them the corresponding steps. Soon, short key-word reminders that are purely instructional, such as cinch, pluck-up, and scooch, will be all that is necessary to suggest the next step. As the story fades away, the child is left with a new skill-set.

Kindergarten teachers will find that it is especially necessary to offer some one-on-one help to at least a handful of the children, at which point, peer-learning, if quietly supported, is likely to take off.

You may also want to consider showing the exercise to a few members of the class in advance. You may perhaps choose those who could benefit from an opportunity to develop leadership skills and build confidence. This helps create enthusiasm and makes for a more efficient use of classroom time. Students enjoy teaching one another. Peer-learning stands behind a good deal of actual classroom learning.

For children under 11 years-old, handwork techniques, such as those found in this book, are best introduced by way of real-time, real-space, demonstration, and not directly from a set of instructions or through some type of electronic media. Students 11 and older may find printed matter helpful when used in combination with live instruction.

I have had new students come into my classroom with serious learning challenges who demonstrated a talent for handwork when it was introduced and thereafter dramatically improved in attitude and confidence.

Below is a set of stories that relate directly to techniques you will learn in this book and that serve as a backdrop for the stories and rhymes accompanying particular lessons. This material is intended to help teachers flesh out any narratives they may wish to expand on or create themselves.

The Land of Hand

The Mysterious Land of Hand is filled with folk as honest and hardworking as one might hope to find. There are also many animals, including those of the sea and sky. If you are lucky, you might meet a gnome or a fairy, or even catch a glimpse of a mermaid.

The Fisherman and the Seagull

The fisherman has put out his net in the hopes of catching some fish. Mr. Cat sits nearby and watches the net with curiosity. The fisherman does not linger, because he prefers to spend his time mending fishing nets or being witty with his friends, instead of sitting around all day waiting for a fish.

In his absence, a seagull flies overhead and spies a wiggly fish that is caught in his net.

The bird swoops down and catches the thin, slippery fish in her sharp beak. There is a bit of a struggle and, to prevent the fish from slipping

Children have a natural respect for meaningful work, and handwork thereby cultivates in them a respect for their elders. Technological replacements for a teacher only rob a child of this opportunity for connection. Completely abstract digital manipulations, such as the pushing of buttons, and passive activities, such as staring into screens, however alluring, are essentially meaningless to a developing mind and only further isolate growing children from the real world. Developing practical skills through hands-on experience imbues the ability to cope with a variety of difficulties we encounter in life.

away, the seagull flips it a bit to get a good hold on the top-fin; then away she flies with her meal.

The curious cat moves in closer, wondering if anything is in the net for him. Just then, the fisherman, taking a break from his gabbing, returns to discover that his net is quite empty and all pulled loose, as well. He cinches it up tight and returns to his merry company.

No sooner does he leave than another seagull, with her keen eyesight, sees a fish wiggling in the net. She swoops down to snatch it up. She struggles momentarily to get a good hold on the fish and flies up and away to feed her young.

Again, the curious cat moves in closer just as the fisherman returns and, finding no fish, cinches up his net again.

And so, the story continues: The seagulls help themselves to all the fish they find in the fisherman's net, bringing them back to feed their chicks, all through the fall season. The cat must be getting something out of the arrangement for he is rather fat and lingers nearby. The fisherman however, never does get his catch.

The fisherman provides a story picture later for "Casting Off."

When winter comes the river begins to freeze. The fisherman cuts his net free. He stuffs the net away in its sack for the winter. He pulls the sack tight. As the seagulls fly away south, their shadows pass over the bottom-feeders who slink and burrow away to hide from their sharp eyes.

✳ For the rhyme about The Fisherman and the Seagull, see chapter 4.

The Rogue Sheep
(A Story for Basic Knitting)

(Weave-On)
One fine day, a young shepherdess led her sheep to a fine grazing spot. She hung the hook of her crook on the fence, sat in the shade to rest, and dozed off. She did not notice when one of her sheep strayed away.

When she awoke, she noticed that one sheep was missing. Not wanting to stray too far from the rest of her flock, she only wandered a short distance off, calling there…and calling here…and there…and here…. She called all around. She did not see the lost sheep anywhere, and so, again, she called out there…and here…and there…until she finally came back to where she had started.

Where did she find her wandering sheep but resting under the very same fence where she had been sleeping. So surprised was the shepherdess to see her lost sheep lying there, that she let out a gasp in surprise.

So startled was the sheep by its keeper's cry that it awoke with a start. It pulled itself up onto its feet and stepped up on a rock to make ready to jump. And up it leaped, right over the top of the fence.

It went running off again, with the shepherdess calling after it. By the time the shepherdess returned with that one, the other sheep were all bleating loudly for her.

(Rows)
By the time the exasperated shepherdess had finally gotten them all calmed down, it was getting late and the sheep were eager to be safe in their pen again. As she herded them along toward home, the rogue sheep thought of the water-trough and a bed of straw to lie on, and he did not wait to be let in by the gate. Having discovered the strength of his legs earlier that day, there was no going back. Nearing the gate, the howl of old Brother Wolf could be heard in the distance and reached the ears of the sheep. The rogue sheep pulled back from the others, climbed onto a slab of rock where he steadied himself, and up it leaped, right over the fence, landing in the barnyard.

In the morning the rogue sheep let himself be let out through the gate.

After learning this new trick, all the sheep made it a habit of jumping over the fence in the evening until they were all safely inside the barn. But in the morning, each sheep waited to be let out through the gate.

This shepherdess took care not to sleep on the job after that long day, but the sheep had already learned their new trick.

✳ For the rhyme about the Rogue Sheep, see chapter 5.

Teaching Handwork to Groups of Young Children

When teaching any kind of handwork to young children, it is good to have an assistant, especially one who has a fair degree of experience in the art, as one-on-one help will often be needed. If you teach a class over a period of time, try to establish a rhythm so that students know what to expect.

Starting handwork classes with a fitting verse or song helps to set the tone. It is also recommended to do some basic finger warm-ups.

Each teacher's rhythm will vary, and each class brings something new. The example class presented here is derived from countless observations in classrooms in many different schools over the course of several decades, which were found to have worked well. Any variety of nice verses, nursery rhymes, and songs can be used.

Example of how a class might go

The teacher stands before her class and waits for silence. With her hands, she gestures for the students to rise and join her in saying a verse.

Following the verse there is a brief—five minutes or so—lesson. Depending at what stage the class is, this lesson time might consist of an introduction to a new project or a new skill for a project that is already in progress. This would be a good time to share a new stitch story, if needed. The teacher might use this moment to give a brief craft-related lesson in color, to showcase a handcrafted piece, or even teach a new song relating to the lesson.

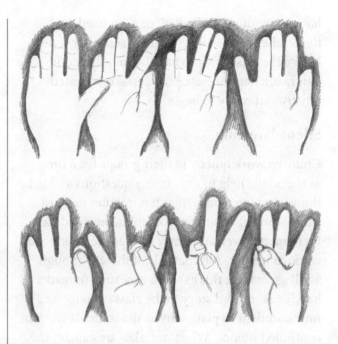

Hand Warm-ups

Following the lesson comes the hand warm-ups. Any basic nursery rhyme or song can be adapted to accompany the finger play for the warm ups. Here are two basic exercises as illustrated above. First, have them spread open the notches between fingers, one-at-a-time. Next, have them bend down each finger in turn to touch the thumb, squeezing them together, then gently rub the tips together in a circular motion: pointer to thumb, middle finger to thumb, ring finger to thumb, and pinky to thumb. It is advisable to start out on one hand and work up to doing the warmups on both hands, as the weeks and months progress. That which seems difficult and even undoable at first, will soon become fluid. Such movements are helpful training for playing instruments as well.

One trick for a child who has difficulty in doing these exercises, is to have them start with the hands flat against a surface such as a desk or table. After just a few repetitions the hands can accomplish the same movements in the air.

Following the brief warm-ups, the work is brought out. The children's work should have been checked since the previous class and some issues may have been found and noted, or even fixed, by the teacher, who will very briefly share her notes before the class prior to handing out the cloth handwork bags or baskets to each child seated quietly and ready to begin.

Silent Working

Children work quietly in their groups for a time as the adults help to answer any questions and get things moving along. After ten minutes or so of silent working, a song or soft chime may indicate that quiet conversation may now ensue, so long as work continues. Alternatively, if there is enough adult assistance, this can be a nice time to read a handwork-related story to the class or to invite a music student to play softly as the students work in continued silence. When mistakes are caught, the work is undone and redone under guidance.

Troubleshooting

By second grade and beyond, handwork projects, including Bare Hand Knitting, can be mapped-out in large colorful, hand-drawn patterns that are laid out as a reference for students and helpers. The teacher may choose to move around the classroom herself, rather than to have the students jumping up when assistance is needed. Some teachers sit at the desk and have the children come up to have problems solved.

As the class progresses, so do the projects. Teachers help to troubleshoot problems and assist students. It is advisable to have a "go-to" activity such as a chain-knitting project available to every child for those occasions when a student runs into a break in the work, for whatever reason. Little by little, week-by-week, a quiet enthusiasm builds as colorful and challenging, satisfying, projects are brought to completion.

Closing

As the lesson comes to an end, the teacher plays a few familiar notes on her chimes, or otherwise gently gives notification, and the children work a bit longer to bring their work to a good resting place. One by one, the children return their projects to their bags or baskets. A student leader can now be chosen from each group or row to collect the handwork bags. The teacher might lead a final song as the bags are passed in and students make ready for the closing verse.

Knitting puts us into a meditative state. It calms the mind and opens a space deep within, where healing can occur. A state such as this offers an opportunity. To what extent one is able to utilize this, depends a great deal upon the surroundings as well as the intention of the individual. There is a lot to be said for a therapeutic environment.

I once met a woman who had grown up wearing the items knitted by her mother's own hands. She cherished those memories and decided, in her late thirties, to take up knitting herself. As we conversed over lunch, at a wool festival in Northern California, she also went on to share that her mother had suffered from anxiety. The two pictures just didn't go together and, almost before the thought had formed, a question left my lips "Did your mother knit while watching the evening news?" I asked. "Yes, every evening, that is what she did!" Why didn't this answer surprise me?

The moment of creating new pathways for thought leaves us open, and there is an inherent vulnerability in this openness. What constitutes a healing environment may differ somewhat from one person to the next and could be approached as a topic all on its own. Some universal themes to work with would be safety, calmness, warmth, beauty, nature, song, and joy. If healing for the mind is what you seek, there is medicine to be had in handwork.

chapter two
Getting Started

Geography of the Hand

To become acquainted with terms used to describe specific areas on your hand, let us take a closer look: Open flat your left hand against your lap or a table. Imagine that this hand is an island, 20 miles wide, floating in the sea. There are several thousand inhabitants on this island, living in villages or scattered cottages about the countryside. In the bays and inlets, fishing boats are anchored.

The inhabitants have names for the important geographical features for their island. These names are capitalized, just as we capitalize the distinctive locations in the regions where we live. There are five distinct peninsulas, named: Thumb, Pointer, Middler, Ringa, and Pinky. There are bays and inlets that have the names of: Thumb-Notch, Arrow-Notch, Center-Notch, and Pinky-Notch.

There is a great central plain where field crops are grown, called Palm. There is a narrow valley that runs from notch-to-notch across the bases of the peninsulas, called the Finger-Palm Crease.

In Bare Hand Knitting, our hands are our tools, and we must have a simple and obvious terminology for describing their interplay with the yarn. Many of the terms used are mapped out below, and some of them may be already familiar to you. Others we have had to invent. Still others will appear as needed.

Throughout the book we must designate individual fingers. The Thumb, Pointer, and Pinky all have simple, well-known names, but the designations for middle finger and ring finger are wordier and, in fact, could waste a good deal of extra ink just printing the word "finger" a few thousand times—not to mention loss of simplicity and clarity. Therefore, for these two fingers, we take the liberty of using obvious nicknames: The middle finger, we shorten to "Middler," and the ring

finger to "Ringa." ("Middler" also distinguishes it from "middle," a word we might sometimes use in instructions.) Here is how we designate our fingers:

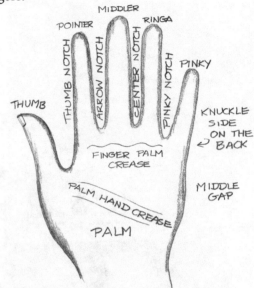

Moving around the Hand

Palm-side:	inside of the hand
Pad-side:	palm-side or inside of the finger
Knuckle-side:	back or knuckle-side of the finger
Thumb-Notch:	where Thumb and Pointer join
Arrow-Notch:	where Pointer and Middler join
Center-Notch:	where Middler and Ringa join
Pinky-Notch:	where Ringa and Pinky join
Finger-Palm Crease:	the arched crease between fingers & palm

If an inhabitant wants to say he is traveling along the Finger-Palm Crease toward the Pinky, he says he is heading "Pinkywise." If his wife goes in the opposite direction to meet him, she is traveling "Thumbwise."

Thumbwise:	moving in a line from the Pinky to Pointer
Pinkywise:	moving in a line from the Pointer to Pinky
Tipwise:	moving along a digit toward the tip
Wristwise:	moving along a digit toward the wrist

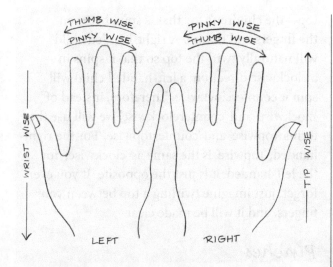

Right and Left Handedness

Whether the reader is right-handed or left-handed, these instructions will work for both. Your dominant hand, we call your "Shuttle Hand," and your passive, or non-dominant hand, is the "Loom Hand." These terms come from weaving, where the loom holds your work and the shuttle moves in and out. In other words, if you are right-handed, your "Shuttle" is your active right hand, while your "Loom" refers to your passive left hand. If you are left-handed, the opposite applies—"Shuttle," in that case, refers to your left hand and "Loom" to your right. Take a moment to get to know your hands by the names I will be addressing them.

Any movement toward the Loom Hand is called Loomwise and movement toward your Shuttle Hand is called Shuttlewise.

In a classroom setting, this terminology clears up confusion by eliminating the necessity of having to give a reversed set of instructions for left-handed students—who will appreciate not being made to feel different. With this system, all the children catch on with no problem. This is the terminology used throughout this book, except for certain chapters on two-hand techniques, where both hands are equally active, and it is easier and more to the point to signify "Left" and "Right" to identify the hands when they are held side-by-side.

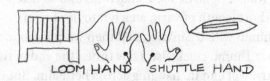

Shuttlewise: moving in a Loom-to-Shuttle direction

Loomwise: moving in a Shuttle-to-Loom direction

(These directional terms are independent of any fixed location. Stitches on your Shuttle Hand can move Shuttlewise because they are moving along an arrow going from Loom to Shuttle.)

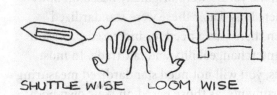

29

Clockwise & Counterclockwise

If Rita, a right-handed student, is told to take a short length of yarn, attach it to her Loom Thumb with a slipknot, and then wrap it around that Thumb clockwise a few times, the end of the yarn will end up hanging across her Palm. But if Lenny, a left-handed student, followed the same instruction, the yarn-end would hang down the back of his hand, behind his Thumb-Notch.

To go along with Loom and Shuttle, a rotational designation is needed that automatically adjusts for left- and right-handed children. Here is the solution: imagine picking up a small spindle-

top—the children's toy that is spun between the fingers and thumb. A right-handed child will naturally twirl the top so that it spins in a clockwise direction; a left-handed child will spin it counterclockwise. Therefore, instead of 'clockwise' and 'counterclockwise' we will use the terms 'topwise' and 'countertopwise.' For the right-handed, 'topwise' is the same as 'clockwise;' for the left-handed, it is just the opposite. If you ever forget, just imagine twirling a top between your fingers, and it will be made clear.

Pinches

The main pinch that will be used for plucking and holding yarn is the *bird-pinch,* which comes most naturally. As your Bare Hand Knitting progresses, others will be called in for specialized actions.

Bird-pinch: thumb-tip touches tip of Pointer.
Fox-pinch: thumb-tip touches tip of Middler

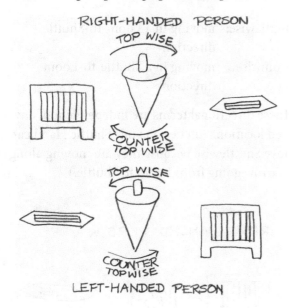

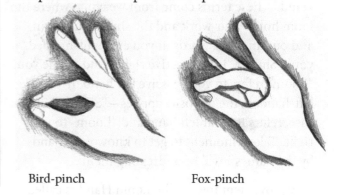

Bird-pinch   Fox-pinch

Measurements

Many common measurements—the inch, the foot, the yard—were originally based on body dimensions. Later these were standardized when there was a need for increased precision for interchangeability and fair trade. In most cases, you will not need standardized measuring instruments, as those based on your own body proportions will serve as well. These individualized measurements are designated with the word *personal:* a *personal inch,* a *personal foot,* a *personal yard.*

Your personal inch can be measured off with the top segment of your thumb.

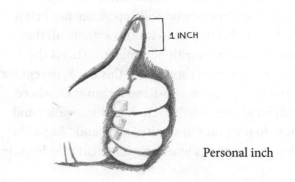

Personal inch

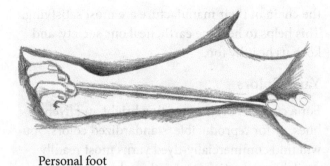

Personal foot

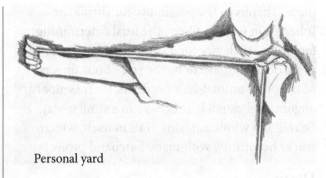

Personal yard

Your personal foot can be measured out by your foot or, perhaps more easily, by the distance from wrist to elbow.

Your personal yard can be measured as the distance from your chin or mid chest, to the tip of the thumb of your outstretched hand. This makes it very easy then, when you want, say, 6 yards of

yarn, to loosely hold the running strand in your off-hand, resting against your chin, while your active hand—your Shuttle Hand— draws out the yarn to the full distance your arm stretches. Draw out the yarn to full length, count one, drop the yarn from your Shuttle Hand and re-pinch it where it emerges from your off-hand, draw it out again—doing this procedure six times.

Choosing Your Materials

"Wool is a special gift to mankind from one of the gentlest animals on earth. For more than 10,000 years, the docility and flocking instincts of sheep have made it one of the most prominent animals in folklore. In ancient times, the sheep were driven through thickets and the fleece was picked off the thorns and gathered for hand spinning."

– *Dana Kraemer*

When choosing materials for a project, it is important to keep in mind that our hands and fingers are continuously in direct skin-contact with the fibers. The naturally-spiraling fibers of wool allow for countless hours of pleasurable,

tactile engagement, with minimal strain. These constant gentle massaging micro-movements have a pleasant and warming effect on the hands. The naturally occurring lanolin in the wool, especially abundant in fisherman's yarn, softens the skin. Using mostly 100% pure wool, and occasionally other rougher fibers such as hemp and linen, even corn husks, raffia, nettle, or recycled silks are preferable.

You can knit for hours on end, year after year, and your fingers and hands will feel better than ever.

At one point, I tried a synthetics/wool mix, but it was unpleasant and had to be abandoned. This is a touch-intensive medium, for which synthetics are not desirable.

Pure and unmixed wool fibers have yet another wonderful attribute: They can be felted down in size, creating an unbroken, thick, soft matted material. Fulling applies the same procedures to a fabric that has first been woven or knitted, giving it flexibility. Fulling results in shrinkage and can be an important final step in the creation of a knitted piece. Thanks to the possibility for shrinkage inherent in woolen fibers, the final determining factor for stitch size for a completed barehand piece does not have to be the size of our fingers. Many other animal-hair products, such as alpaca, angora, and camel hair behave in a similar way. Felting is a whole amazing craft in itself, which works beautifully with many barehand projects.

Decor

Decorative fringes, linings, and such can be added to our pieces using silk ribbons, hemp, linen, cotton, or recycled materials. In general, cotton, silk, hemp, and such yarns are less flexible, and you will want to work up to extensive Bare Hand Knitting with them over time as you learn to work with the extra tension and your hands gain in strength. Fibers vary greatly in this way, and you will find yourself making minute adjustments in how you work with each.

Yarn Thickness

If you want a thin item with larger holes you can use thinner yarn. For thicker and tighter garments use thicker yarn or felt-down the finished piece. Combining several strands of thinner yarn when creating a large piece creates a still different result from that of Bulky or Fluffy yarns. Huge skeins of thin coarse yarn, used for making wool rugs, are probably the least expensive natural material that you will find. This may not seem like a desirable material to use, but it is possible to felt right through the resulting pieces, with fabulous results. Working with thick hemp cordage in certain instances where its qualities are called for—such as for the underside of a large knitting bag—is effective. But staying attentive to the comfort of your hands usually limits working with such coarse fibers to a few hours at a time.

It is good to be aware of the origins of the materials: the fibers, buttons, and beads you use. Products made closer to home and processed without the use of toxic materials or slave labor and those lacking huge smokestack industries in

the chain of their manufacture are most satisfying. This helps to heal the earth, heal our society, and keep us healthy too.

Yarn Colors

For a cheerful project needing bright and lively hues, or for reproducible, standardized colors, you will find commercially-dyed yarns most readily available and satisfactory—though you would be amazed at the variety of colors natural dyes can produce. And artisans are expanding on these techniques every day. When your projects are suited to vibrant, if often milder colors and more varied hues, you might consider plant-dyed or un-dyed yarns, with their warm browns, soft grays, and creamy whites.

Using bulkier yarns when learning new techniques is helpful for overall ease and success.

Once you have mastered a technique, you will enjoy knitting with all sizes of yarns, making the necessary adjustments to your tensions on a fine motor level almost without thinking about it.

Yarn Sizes

Universally accepted yarn sizes have been designated as follows:
1. Super Fine (also called Sock, Fingering, and Baby)
2. Fine (also called Sport and Baby)
3. Light (also called DK and Light-Worsted)
4. Medium (also called Worsted, Afghan, and Aran)
5. Bulky (also called Chunky, Craft, and Rug)
6. Super Bulky (also called Bulky and Roving)

Sources for Wool

Fiber Shed is an organization that can help connect knitters to local suppliers of yarn and wool. A list of Fiber Shed locations is included in the back of this book. Look for upcoming wool festivals in your local area, where you can buy directly from local suppliers. Also, check out your local yarn shop.

For larger amounts of yarn, you can often get discounts when buying directly from suppliers in bulk. Several handwork teachers order in bulk at a discount from Brown Sheep Co., which carries 100% wool yarn from US sheep. Thrift stores will often have some new skeins available; check them out from time to time.

And, if you really get serious: before you get totally swept away with the enchantment of Bare Hand Knitting, you might even want to take up spinning! There may be a group in your area, where you can learn the skill, as well as find new sources of wool.

Rolling a Ball of Yarn

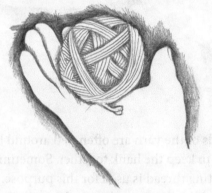

To roll a ball of yarn is really a lovely activity. The circular movements involved have a calming effect. In the kindergarten classroom, there would sometimes be a whole row of children lined up to roll their yarn balls at story time before their naps. They could hardly wait for their chance to do this and it worked like a charm. As their balls wound up, they wound down. All Bare Hand Knitting begins with a ball of yarn.

Hand-spun yarns come in a hank for storage. To try to knit directly from a hank would spell a disastrous tangle. But even the slick machine-made skeins, or giant yarn-cones for weaving yarn, must first be re-wound into balls for our purposes. Knitting from a ball puts just the right tension into the yarn, keeping our stitches even and helping to prevent tangles.

To roll from a machine-wound spool, you may just want to sit while you form your ball. Generally, the yarn pulls out from the center of the spool. If you have an upright cylinder skein, be sure that you are seated above the spool, in order to prevent the yarn from catching on itself as it is unwound.

Methods for Rolling a Ball of Yarn from a Hank

If you have no one there to help you, here are three good options:

(1) Place two dining-chairs back-to-back so that the posts at the corners of the backs are the right space apart to hold the skein.

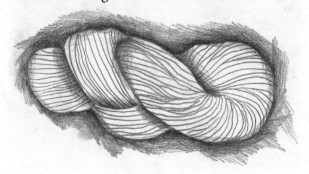

Yarn-Swift

(2) Obtain an age-old device called a yarn-swift, which is specifically-designed to hold a skein in place while you roll.

Barefoot Yarn-Swift

(3) Simply sit flat on the floor with your legs stretched out in front and place the skein across your two feet, spreading them as needed to keep the hank taut, and wind away!

The time-honored method of rolling a ball from a hank involves two people. This brings a social element to our task—but is also actually quite efficient.

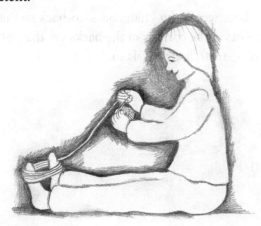

The Team Method

Untwist the skein and open it up. You will be left with a big oval loop of yarn.

Place it on a flat surface in order to remove the skein dividers (most homemade skeins will have threaded divider-points which were put there to prevent tangling and must be severed before you begin to roll).

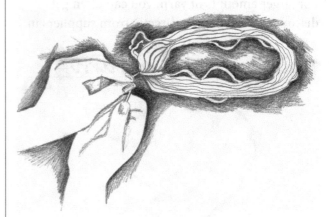

The ends of the yarn are often tied around the loop of yarn to keep the hank together. Sometimes a contrasting thread is used for this purpose. If the yarn itself has been used to tie the yarn together, you'll want to gently untie those knots. If you find this impossible, cut the yarn as close to the knot as possible making sure you don't cut your working yarn in the process.

Begin by having your helper hold out their arms as if they were about to give you a big hug. Hang the yarn skein on your helper's arms.

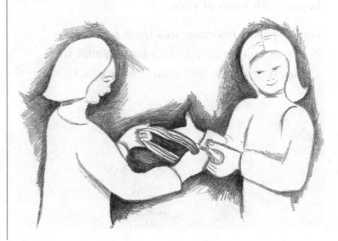

Taking up the yarn with your Shuttle Hand, pinch the end between the fingers of your Loom Hand, and then start rolling it around your whole Loom Hand.

Wind in one direction, around your hand about 6 times.

Slip the clump of yarn off your hand and continue to roll, but now crosswise to the strands, roughly the same number of times.

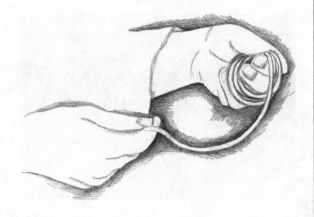

Twist it at the middle forming the shape of an 8.

Fold it back over itself to form a circle again.

Continue wrapping the yarn around and around, rotating the ball as you go, to make a nice even ball. Do not wind the yarn too tight, as you do not want to overstretch the fibers. Continue until the yarn is all wound up.

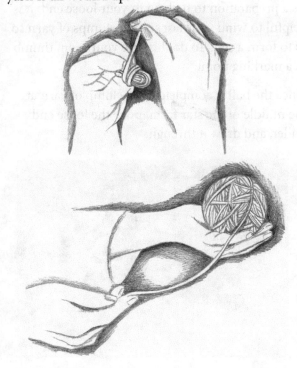

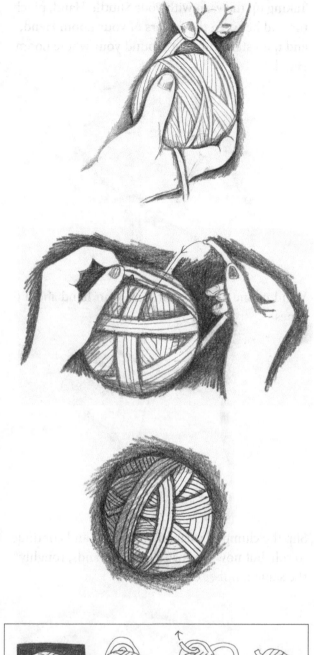

Your assistant can help the process by slowly rocking their arms back and forth tracing a figure eight in the air while moving each hand in a small circle to aid the yarn in slipping off. Most of these movements will come naturally to you both as you work together as a team.

Tucking in Your Ends

Always keep your balls of yarn with the ends tucked under when not in use—it is amazing the trouble that can be caused by loose ends!

As a preparation to tucking in your loose end, it is helpful to wind your last several clumps of yarn so as to form a star. To do this, use your loom thumb as a marking point.

Once the ball is complete, lift a clump of yarn at the middle of the star form, poke the loose end under, and draw it through.

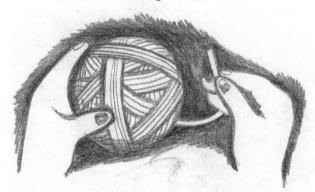

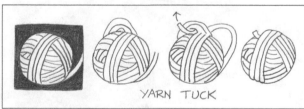

YARN TUCK

Yarn Terminology

Working-yarn: The strand of yarn between your work and the yarn-ball. As we work, we unroll this yarn from the ball and stitch it into our work.

Leed: A synonym for, and meaning exactly the same as, "working-yarn." Working barehanded, we are constantly referring to the working-yarn itself, rather than knitting needles or crochet hooks, we have a need for this simple, shorter word that means the same as "working-yarn." Although *leed* is derived from and similar in meaning to the word "lead" that is pronounced the same way, we spell it differently in this craft to avoid confusion. ("Lead" is a word that already comes with a confusing burden of meanings and pronunciations.)

Tail: The short strand hanging from your work opposite the Ball-Side, later to be woven back into the work.

Dangler or **Dangling-End**: The remaining strand hanging from your knitted piece after the working strand has been cut, either to switch colors, to end the work, or for any other purpose.

Loose End: The outer end on a ball of yarn, which should be kept tucked in.

Bight: A bend or loop or half-loop created in the middle—rather than at one end—of a strand of yarn or rope. This is a common nautical term.

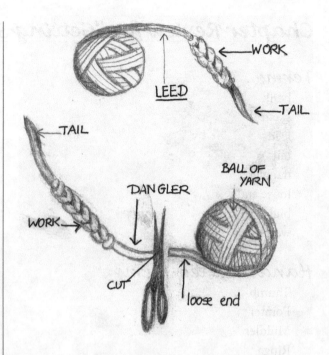

Wherever possible we have used traditional knitting terms, but in some cases new terms had to be created for this medium. In the vocabulary review at the end of each chapter, you will find a listing of newly introduced terms that will be built upon in future chapters. New concepts will be placed in the following categories and in this order:

Knitting Terms

Operations: specific movements relating to Bare Hand Knitting

Elements: individual moves (likened to letters)

Stitches: made up of one or two elements (likened to words)

Polystitches: groups of elements or stitches in a certain order (likened to sentences)

Sequences: longer grouping of stitches or polystitches (likened to paragraphs)

Rows: repeating series of stitches or polystitches (likened to lists)

Chapter Review for "Getting Started"

Terms
hank
skein
leed
tail
dangler
loose end
bight
weave

Hand-Related Terms
Thumb
Pointer
Middler
Ringa
Pinky
Bird-pinch
Fox-pinch
Coyote-pinch
Peacock-pinch

Barehand Geography
Thumb-Notch
Arrow-Notch
Center-Notch
Pinky-Notch
Palm
Finger-Palm Crease
Palm-side
Pad-side

Definitions
Bird-Pinch: Thumb-tip touches tip of Pointer.
Fox-Pinch: Thumb-tip touches tip of Middler

Directions
Pinkywise
Thumbwise
topwise
countertopwise
in
out

Body-Based Measurements
personal yard
personal foot
personal inch

chapter three
Braiding and Knotting

Braiding is a simple and beautiful method for entwining long pieces together. The braiding or plaiting of hair is just one of its many uses. Head crowns can be braided from vines and stems, belts can be braided from fibers and cloth of all kinds. A braid gathers its parts together in a decorative pattern. This technique can be learned at a very young age. In cozy warm kitchens, children can learn to braid with strips of dough, forming beautiful loaves of fresh-baked bread.

"The Flying Fish" A Story for Braiding

One day, when the ocean was warm and flat, a young boy named Gabriel was wading near the shore, waist deep. He watched as a school of silver fish approached, gliding toward him like a shimmering cloud. Suddenly, he heard a quick series of flapping sounds on the surface of the water, flip, flap, flip, flap. The entire school of fish had in a moment leapt into the air, only to splash back down again. They did this with perfect fluidity.

The boy watched in awe as the shimmering school of fish moved away from him. Still evenly spaced and moving in perfect symmetry. Gabriel thought to himself, "I wonder how all those little fishes flew through the air and landed together again, without bumping into each other or getting mixed up." How he loved to watch them go by!

And as he braided the edges of his fishing nets, Gabriel had only to remember the fluid movements of the silvery fish, as they flew up out of the water at brief intervals, only to land back, splash, and swim under water again.

Up out of the water, then splash, back under the water again.

Braiding

Prepare three strings for a practice piece.

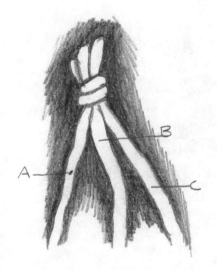

Lift A, moving shuttlewise pass over B, set down between B and C.

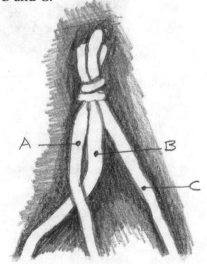

Lift C moving loomwise pass over A, set down between A and B.

Lift C moving shuttlewise move under B. Then repeat these steps for full braid.

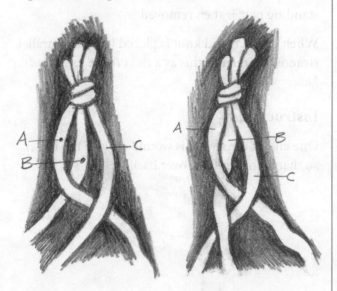

Knots

Here you will be introduced to some basic knots, all of which are used in this book. You will learn the *lark's head knot*, the *overhand knot*, the *square knot*, the *bow knot,* and the *magic knot.* The *slipknot* is introduced in chapter four. Sets of instructions for other knots may or may not be shown with the hands making them, depending on whether a view of the hands doing the work seems helpful or distracting. Once each knot is introduced, step by step, all of the knotting instructions are distilled into a simplified illustration sequence, which is used wherever the knot is called for throughout the book. Many of the knots will require adult assistance for young children doing the projects using them. Learning a new kind of knot is like learning a new word. You will suddenly notice the surprising frequency of its use and an opportunity for its application may present itself at any time.

Let's begin with a review of some standard knot terms that may be used anywhere in the book.

Standard Knot Terms

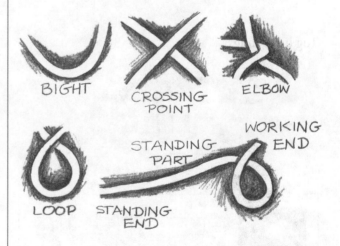

Lark's Head Knot

This knot is commonly used in macramé to attach one strand at right angles to another. It is one of the quickest and easiest knots to learn.

Instructions

In our example pictured below, we are attaching a single strand to a double strand. Double the single strand, forming a bight, and slip the loop of the bight under the doubled strand.

Pinching the ends of the single strand together, wrap them over the doubled strands and thread them through the loop.

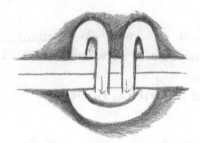

Tug until snug.

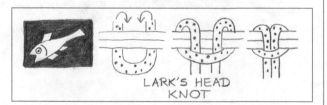

LARK'S HEAD KNOT

Overhand Knot

The *overhand knot*, also called a *single knot*, uses a separate standing part, such as the hand or a finger to wrap around, for the creation of the knot. This standing part is then removed.

When an overhand knot is placed into two parallel strands, we refer to this as a *two-strand overhand knot*.

Instructions

One end of the strand is wound around the finger so that it crosses back over itself.

One end is then tucked into and drawn through the loop.

Tug until snug.

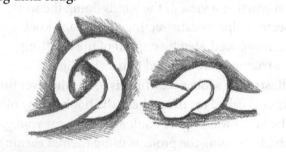

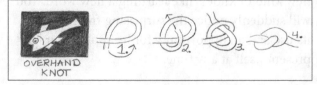

OVERHAND KNOT

Two-Strand Overhand Knot

This knot is a simple and strong way to join two strands.

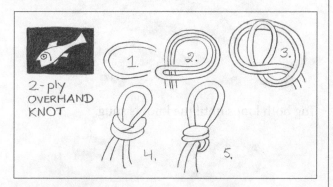

Square Knot

A *square knot*, also called a *reef knot*, is one way to tie two yarn-ends together. It is also sometimes referred to as a *full knot,* as it is comprised of two *half knots*; a half-knot being the first step when you begin to tie your shoelaces in a bow knot.

It doesn't matter which end comes out on top when you make the first half-knot, but when you tie the second half-knot on top, make sure the strands on the left emerge either both going over or both go under the loop, so that they lie neatly alongside each other. The same goes for the strands on the right.

To practice you will need two strands. It helps is they are different colors. We will call the strand which starts on your shuttle side, strand A which is dotted and the strand that starts on the Loom side and is plain, strand B.

Instructions

Make a half-knot by wrapping strand A over, under and back up from strand B.

Make a crossing of the two strands A and B and wrap them under each other in such a way that when one end goes to the left and the other to the right, the strands on the right pass either both over or both under the loop. The same for the leftmost strands. A little ditty to keep it going in the right direction is: "Right over left and under; left over right and under."

Strand A and strand B are tugged until the square knot is snug.

Practice the square knot a few times, and you will soon get the hang of it.

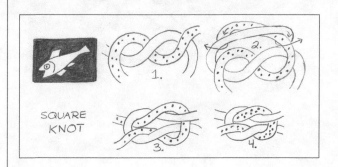

Bow Knot

Also referred to as the *rabbit-ears knot*, this knot offers a commonly used method for tying shoelaces. It starts out with a half knot just as does the square knot and any number of other knots.

Instructions

Make a half -knot as with the square knot.

Strands A and B are now folded over to form loops.

Bring loop A forward over loop B, down and back out through the open space between the two loops.

Tug both loops until the knot is snug.

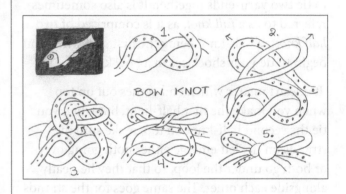

Magic Knot

This knot is known as the magic knot because it simply cannot be pulled out. This is the knot I like to use for thinner yarns or the stiffer and more slippery yarns of hemp and linen and silk.

You may have had the experience of wearing Chinese finger cuffs on your fingers and found that the harder you pull, the tighter they get. This knot works by the same principle. Because the tensions are moving in opposite directions, tugging at the knot only serves to strengthen it, rather than to loosen it. For this knot to work, it must be done exactly right. It is a tricky knot to learn but once you have it down it is ever so useful. Because of the level of complexity and the sense of direction required, I would not ask young children to struggle with this knot, but rather do it for them.

The magic knot can be used to do yarn-changes where a felt splice is either not possible or unwanted. The knot is very secure and can hardly be seen. It works well for *alternating plain-and-chain* (chapter 6) because, unlike other knots, it is smooth enough to chain-knit through.

Instructions

To attach a new thread of yarn onto your working yarn, follow these steps:

Find a flat surface to work on. Leave 8 inches of working yarn—strand A. Place new strand B parallel alongside strand A.

Thread strand B under strand A, curve over to the right over strand A and under itself.

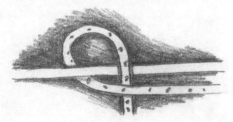

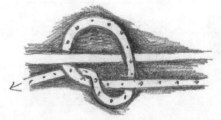

Thread strand B to the left over and under the same strand and pull to the left. Notice that strand B is still on the same side as originally placed.

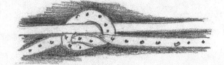

Pull semi snug.

Repeat this process with strand A, only this time the knot will be the opposite of the first knot.

The two knots should be next to each other. Tug on the old strand A and the new strand B simultaneously and the two knots will draw together and snug-up nicely.

45

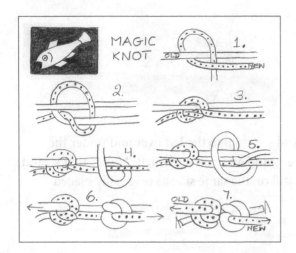

Test out your knot by tugging firmly on the long strands on either side of the new knot. If the knot is secure, you have done everything properly and may cut the two dangling ends right up close to your magic knot.

Slipknot

The *slipknot* will be explained in the following chapter and lead directly to finger knitting.

chapter four
Finger-Knitting a Chain

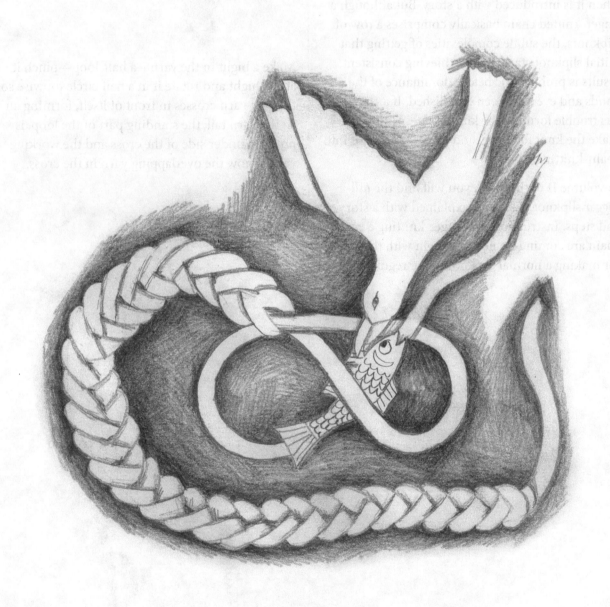

Making a slipknot is the first step for many types of knitting, including chain knitting, and many of the more advanced barehand techniques. Most adults already know how to make a slipknot, but many children today have never learned the most basic of knots such as this one. For young children, the slipknot can be elusive, although kindergartners can do quite well with chain-knitting, especially when it is introduced with a story. But although a finger-knitted chain basically comprises a row of slipknots, the subtle complexities of getting that initial slipknot started and achieving consistent results is problematic before dominance of the hands and eyes has been established. If a child has trouble forming the knot, it doesn't hurt to make the knot for them, and let them go right into chain-knitting.

In volume II of this book you will find the *tail-tugger* slipknot technique explained with a story and steps. Instructions for finger-knitting a yarn-chain are coming up next, so begin with the steps for making a normal slipknot in the regular way.

First Step: The Slipknot

To practice, take up the loose end of a ball of yarn.

Make a bight in the yarn—a half-loop—pinch it at the bight and rotate it in a half circle topwise so that the yarn crosses in front of itself, forming an x. The yarn tail, the standing part of the loop, is now the under side of the cross and the working yarn is now the overlapping yarn in the cross.

With your Loom Hand, pinch the cross to secure it.

Using your Shuttle Hand, poke an inverted U of the working strand up through the loop.

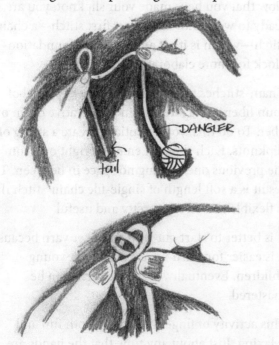

Gently tug at the top of the new loop, and a knot called the *base knot* will tighten at the collar of the new loop.

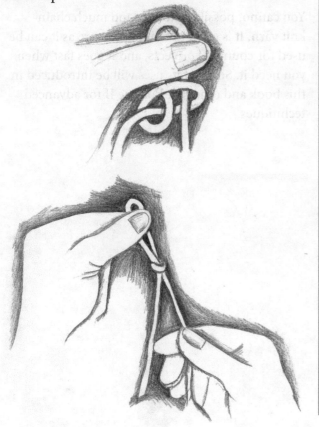

✳ You have just created a slipknot!

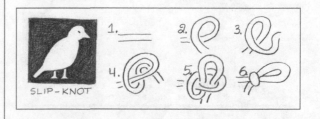

Now that you have created a slipknot, practice it a few times, until it comes naturally to you. Before proceeding to the chain stitch, you will also want to familiarize yourself with the mechanics of adjusting the size of your loop.

You will find that if the loop is too big, you tug at the working-yarn in order to make it smaller.

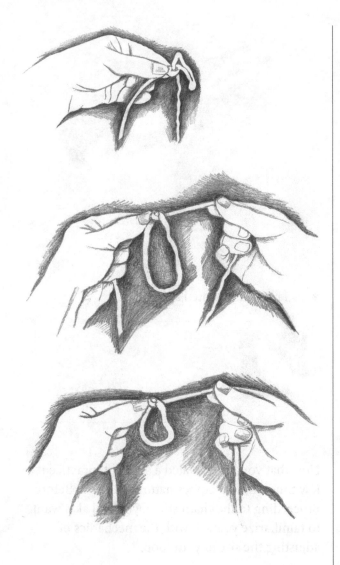

Finger-Knitting a Row of Chain

Now that you have made your slipknot, you are ready to work into it for your first stitch—a chain stitch—which is itself an important foundation-block for more elaborate techniques.

Chain-stitches transform an ordinary strand of spun fiber into a stretchy and decorative chain of fiber. To do this, you essentially create a string of slipknots. Each slipknot emerges right out from the previous one, leaving no space in between. The result is a soft length of single-file chain-stitch that is flexible and strong, pretty and useful.

It is better to start out with a thicker yarn because it is easier for learning, especially for young children. Eventually, even fine yarns can be mastered.

This activity of finger knitting is both fun and relaxing. Just about any time that the hands are free is a fine time for the production of this useful material. My favorite time to practice finger knitting is on my morning walks.

You cannot possibly produce too much chain-knit yarn. It is good to build up a store as it can be used for countless projects, and it goes fast when you need it. Some of its uses will be introduced in this book and others in Volume II for advanced techniques.

If the loop is too small, tug on the side of the loop that is closest to the working-yarn to enlarge it.

If you tug on the side that is closest to the tail, you will tighten the base of the loop instead.

This wonderful knot allows for easy slippage of the yarn strand through it. The size of the loop is adjustable and, once secured around something (even just another strand), a slipknot will not come undone. The knot is as strong as the fibers from which it is formed.

Rhyme for Chain-Knitting

The fisherman fixes his net;
Creep close, little kitty, but do not get wet!
See a Seagull dive in,
Snatch a fish by the fin—
But what will the fisherman get?

– A. Akin

Instructions for Chain-Knitting

Set-Up

Find a comfortable place to sit and place the yarn-ball to your Shuttle side. Use Medium- to Bulky-sized wool yarn for learning-practice.

Create a slipknot with a loop about the size of the girth of your thumb.

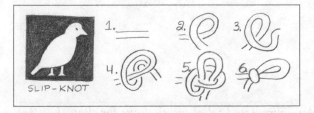

Grip just below the slipknot with your Loom bird-pinch.

Note: Getting a good hold on this spot becomes easier once the first few stitches accumulate, because you will then be holding a knitted chain, instead of just the thin strand.

Bend the loop down over the leed—as if the loop were a magnifying glass through which you were examining it.

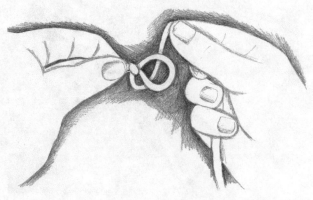

Pass through the loop with your Shuttle bird-pinch and pluck the leed, drawing it back up through into a new loop.

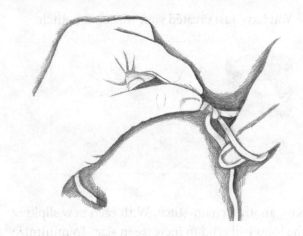

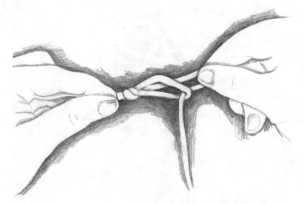

Tug gently at this new loop until it is snug at its base.

Scoot your Loom bird-pinch up a notch closer to the loop.

＊ You have just created your first chain-stitch.

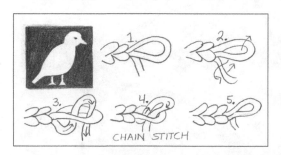

Knit another chain-stitch. With each new slipknot the loop will tend to increase in size. To minimize this, stop, and then tug at the top of the emerging new loop, rather than just pulling at its front.

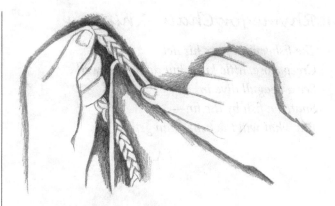

Adjust the size, if necessary, in preparation for your next stitch.

Continue to knit chain-stitches until the desired length is accomplished.

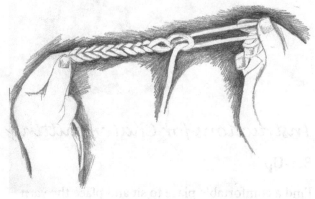

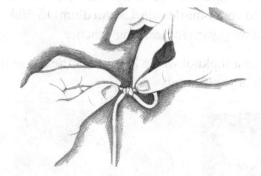

An abbreviated set of instructions for chain-knitting using key words as a handy teaching reference can be found in the chapter review, under "Stitches."

When you are ready to end your knitted chain, secure your stitches from unraveling by doing as follows:

Tie-Off

Cut the yarn strand about six inches from the last stitch. Once it has been severed, the leed emerging from the knitted piece becomes the dangler.

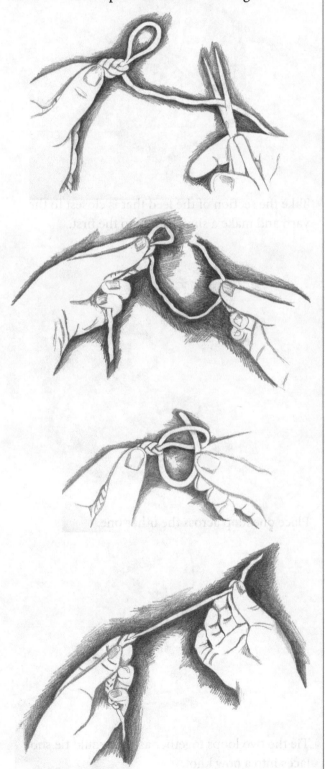

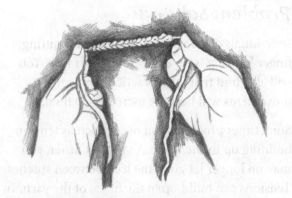

Remember to tuck in the loose end on your yarn ball. Do this by pushing it under several secure strands on the ball. This is an important practice that will prevent time-consuming tangles.

✳ You have just completed your first tie-off sequence.

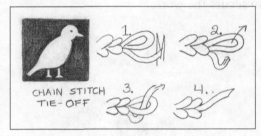

Weaving-In the Dangler

To conceal the tail and/or the dangler, you can weave it back into your knitted chain.

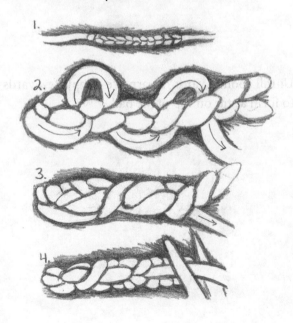

Problem Solving

Individuals develop varying styles for knitting; finger knitting is no exception to this rule. You will also find that with practice, your micro-movements will become increasingly fluid.

Sometimes problems can occur such as tension building up in the work. As you get faster, you may no longer let go of the leed between stitches. Tensions can build up in the fibers of the yarn. In this case your work is likely to become wound up as you go. If this happens, you can wind down the tensions.

Releasing Tensions

Place the last loop of your chain on the Loom Thumb to secure the work.

Unroll about 3 yards of yarn. Re-wrap a few yards to form a star on top of the ball.

Push a section of the leed under the star, pulling through an 8- inch double strand.

Take the section of the leed that is closest to the yarn and make a similar loop to the first.

Place one loop across the other one.

Tie the two loops together as you would tie shoe laces into a bow knot.

Tie them together again into a double knot.

Dangle the ball of yarn by the leed and watch the ball spin to unwind the tension.

Undo the knot to free up the working yarn. Return to chain-knitting.

To prevent this from occurring in the future, you can simply alternate the angle and direction of pulling through each new loop. To paddle a canoe in a straight direction, paddle first on one side and next on the other. The same is true for finger-knitting a chain. You will quickly become accustomed to this slight adjustment to your technique.

Connecting a Circular Chain

To make a circular chain that connects back on itself, use a felt meld. This method is called for in several fun projects for this chapter.

To begin with, be sure that the very first stitch of your chain is not tugged too tight.

loosen up

When your chain is the desired length, cut the yarn leaving an 8-inch-long dangler—but do not tie-off.

Place the last loop of your chain up through the first stitch of your chain and push the dangler upwards through that loop.

Push the dangler up through the loop.

Push the tail through that same loop.

Tug at the dangler and tail to snug-up the knot.

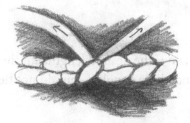

Hiding the Ends

Tie a small overhand knot at the tip of the tail and the dangler.

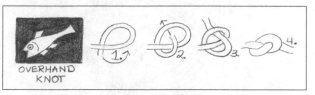

Weave the dangler in and out of the starting side of the chain and weave the tail in and out through the ending side of the chain, until only an inch is left unwoven, on each.

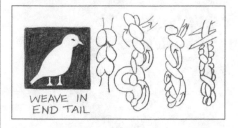

Completed weave-in.

Snip off the knots at each end.

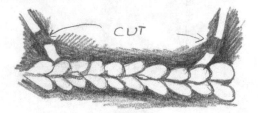

Wet the woven-through length of chain with a splash of water and a dot of soap and roll it between the palms of your hands, until the fibers are warm with friction.

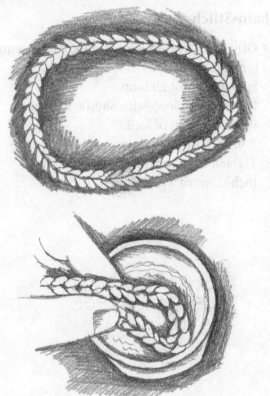

Do this several times until the tail and dangler have "melded" into the work and no longer show.

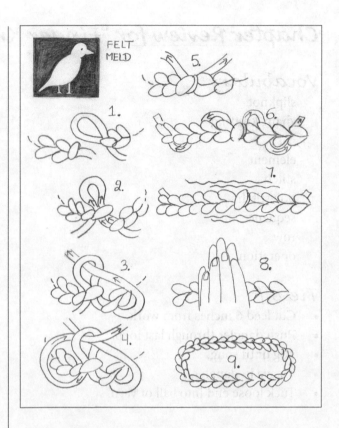

✻ You have created a felt meld.

Variations

Depending upon your purpose for knitting a chain, you may want to pull your stitches more tightly or loosely. A tight chain will have more elasticity, whereas a looser chain has a smooth appearance. If you intend to weave-in the tail and dangler, remember not to pull the stitches too tight.

Chapter Review for "Finger Knitting a Chain"

Vocabulary

   slipknot
   chain-knitting
   base
   element
   stitch
   polystitch
   sequence
   row
   operation

Tie-off

- Cut leed 6 inches from work.
- Push dangler through last loop.
- Tug until snug.
- Weave in dangler.
- Tuck loose end into ball of yarn.

Stitches

Chain-Stitch

- Grip yarn beneath base of slipknot in Loom bird-pinch.
- Spot leed through loop.
- Pass through loop with Shuttle bird-pinch.
- Pluck-up bight of leed.
- Pull back through loop.
- Tighten from top, till base knot is snug.
- Inch forward with Loom bird-pinch.

Projects for Finger-Knitting a Chain

Substituting alternative yarns for patterns may alter your measurements. Yarn made with 100% wooly animal fibers (except when another fiber is called for) is necessary for optimal results and in some cases will affect the functional success of a given project.

Yarn Jewelry

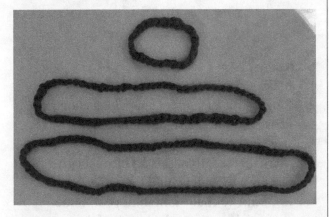

Materials

You will want to have about 1/4th of a skein—or 24 personal yards—of Burly spun 100% wool yarn, to make all three items: a necklace, a bracelet, and a hair tie. Also, have a splash of water and a spot of soap handy.

Steps

1. Make a slipknot and place it on Pointer.
2. Finger-knit a chain of a length to fit your project (leave the first stitch a tad loose in preparation for a felt meld.)
   - For a *necklace* it should at least fit over your head, at a slight stretch.
   - For a *bracelet* it should fit over your hand, at a slight stretch.
   - For a *hair tie* the length of the chain should be just long enough to fit around your head and the nape of your neck, snug enough that it would stay on at a slight stretch, but not too tight.

3. Do a felt meld. (This step, a felt meld, only works with real wool yarn. If you are using other fibers, at this point you can simply tie the two ends to each other with a square knot and weave-in the ends.)

Variations

To make a fancy hairband, select matching or complementing colors and materials for any additional ribbons or yarns you might add for decor. Adding a Pom-Pom can work nicely as a ponytail-tie or key-chain or a zipper-tug. As a final variation to the above project, using raffia, instead of wool yarn, you can create a nice base for a flower head-garland for May Day. Simply finger-knit a chain of a length to fit loosely around the crown of your head. Be sure that you leave long enough stems on your flowers to poke them in through one stitch and back out through the next. Have fun and good luck!

Magic Rope for Creative Dress-up

Various lengths of twice-knit chain yarn can be a truly wonderful resource for creative play. It is both useful and versatile. Just throw in some colorful material and sprinkle a bit of childhood imagination and it becomes like "magic rope." Tell the children some good stories and watch the play develop. You will be amazed by what can arise

from the imagination with a few simple props to spark it. You will find specific projects for this, in the projects section, for this chapter.

Dress-up Desert Headdress

Materials

- You will need 1/16 of a skein (8.5 personal yards length) of Burly wool yarn.
- A square or rectangular cut of cloth large enough to fit over the top of the head and hang over the sides.

Steps

1. Make a slipknot.
2. Finger-knit a length of chain long enough to fit around the crown of your head, at a slight stretch.
3. Mark that length of this set of stitches by placing a tell-tail behind the active stitch.
4. Continue to chain-knit until your knitted chain is three times the length of the first set of stitches, then add an additional 8 inches.
5. Cut the yarn and tie-off.
6. Create a slipknot 4 inches from the tail of finger-knitted chain and place it on your Loom Pointer. This is making a double-chain.
7. Finger-knit the chain a second time, pulling each stitch snug, leaving an 8-inch dangler of chain.
8. Poke the last loop of double-chain through the initial one and draw the leed through it.
9. Push the tail up through the second-to-last stitch of the chain.
10. Tie-off the tail and the dangler with a tight double square knot.
11. Place cloth on head and pull turban holder around the cloth and around the crown of the head to secure it on.

Play Horsie-Bridle

Materials

You will need about 2½ skeins—475 yards of Bulky wool yarn.

Steps

1. Make a slipknot.
2. Finger-knit all 475 yards into chain. (This will result in about 158 yards of chain.)
3. Tie-off.
4. Finger-knit the chain a second time, pulling each stitch snug, leaving a four-inch dangler of chain.
5. Tie-off.
6. Fold the length of twice-knit chain in half.
7. Measure one personal yard from the bight in your twice-knit chain and tie it off with an overhand knot.

Play-Belt with Hilt

Materials

You will need about one skein—190 yards of Bulky wool yarn.

Steps

1. Make a slipknot.
2. Finger-knit all 190 yards. (This will give you about 63 yards of chain.)
3. Tie-off.
4. Finger-knit the chain a second time, pulling each stitch snug, leaving a four-inch dangler of chain, giving you a length of chain rope.

Tying-Off the Hilt

1. Hang the chained-rope around your shoulders so that the mid-point is at the back of your neck. The two sides should be hanging down the front of your body, with the ends coming to the same point.
2. Tie the two strands together with a two-strand overhand knot, just at the height of the belly button.
3. Tie a second two-strand overhand knot four inches from the first, toward the rope ends, creating a slit between the two knots.

Wearing the Rope

The first loop goes over the torso, sideways. The second loop sits at the hip, to hold a sword. The rope-ends are then tied around the waist to secure the belt. A sword can now be slid into the slit at the hip.

chapter five
Basic Hand Knitting

Knitting on one hand is the amazing and surprisingly efficient process through which spun fiber is transformed into a loose springy fabric, the rows of which appear to stream out from the back of your hand as you work. By continually lifting loops of yarn over the working yarn, essentially pulling loops from within loops upon multiple fingers, you will produce a piece that, once cast off, naturally curls in on both sides, giving it a tubular appearance.

Any of a number of natural, flexible, and touch-friendly yarns can be used for this technique. If the yarn is bulky, a tighter piece will result. Choose a medium-to-bulky-weight wool yarn while you are learning.

Like finger-knitting, the art of basic hand knitting can be practiced just about any time that the hands are free. Once learned, it becomes a relatively pleasant pastime that can easily accompany a conversation or a walk.

Knitting on One Hand

Rhyme for Easy Knitting on One Hand

The shepherdess ties up her sack;
Her little lost sheep she must track:
Out and in and out and around,
Out and in and out and around,
Just to find him asleep in her track.
Crying out, she awakens her sheep.
He is raised to his feet with a bleat,
Oh, what a joy,
The rogue sheep has been found!
But right over the fencing he leaps.

Rows
You must know that where sheep are concerned,
Such behavior is easily learned:
What the first sheep will do,
All the others will too,
The whole flock jumps the fence now, in turn.

Cast-Off
From now on, the sheep leap the home gate;
But come morning are led out to graze.
The rest follow in turn,
Even Lambie can learn—
Please tie off the gate to be safe.
– A. Akin

Creating a Hair-Tie

Set-Up
Find a comfortable place to sit and place the yarn ball to one side, draping the tail of yarn across your lap.

The Palm-Heart Position

The Palm-Heart position gives a uniform starting place for most of the projects. Usually, there will be a reference to the Loom Hand: To find proper placement, simply place your Loom Hand on your chest and then pull it away from the chest about a hand-span's distance—six inches or so.

In this position, your palm faces your heart and your thumb is sticking more-or-less straight up.
✻ You are now in Palm-Heart Position.

PALM HEART

Weave-On

Pick up the strand with your Shuttle Hand, about six inches from the end, and bring it up between your Loom Hand and your chest and drape it through the Thumb-Notch letting the tail fall down the back of your hand.

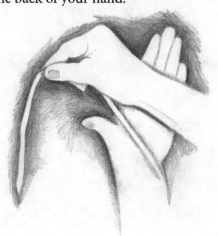

Using your Shuttle Hand, pluck the yarn at the palm-side of your Thumb-Notch and wind it three times, topwise, around your Loom Thumb to anchor it.

Weave the leed in and out between your fingers, in Pinkywise direction, as follows:

With your Loom Hand still in Palm-Heart position, grip the leed with your Shuttle Hand and bring it back through the Arrow-Notch (of your Loom Hand).

Bring the leed toward you again through the Center-Notch.

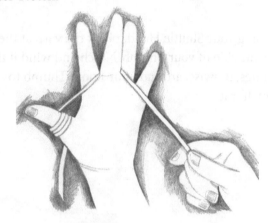

Take the leed back out through the Pinky-Notch.

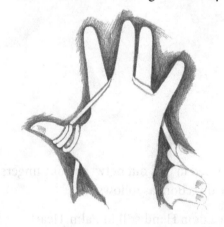

Bring the leed around the outside of Pinky, topwise, toward you.

Weave the leed back again slalom-style, Thumbwise (in the direction toward the Thumb of your Loom Hand), as follows:

Take the leed back through the Pinky-Notch to the knuckle side.

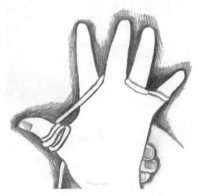

Bring it toward you again through the Center-Notch, to the pad-side.

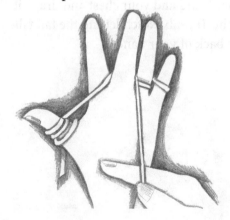

Take the leed back out through the Arrow-Notch.

Finally, bring the leed countertopwise around Pointer, toward you, and lay it across your Palm, Pinkywise.

You will now see a cross at the base of your Pointer, the upright of which is formed by the Leed and the cross-bar of which stretches between your Arrow-Notch and your Thumb, around which it is wrapped.

Using your Shuttle Hand in a bird-pinch, pluck up the cross-bar at the Thumb-side of the upright.

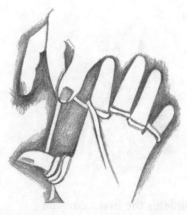

Bring it over the top of Pointer, thus securing the cast-on. (It helps to duck your finger as it passes under the plucked strand.)

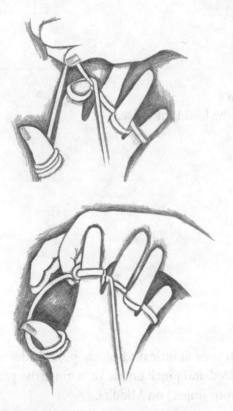

The leed should now be emerging to the palm side of the Arrow-Notch and falling down along your Finger-Palm Crease. If it is hanging from the knuckle-side of the Arrow-Notch instead, then just bring it through the Arrow-Notch to the palm-side.

* This completes the first *weave-on*.

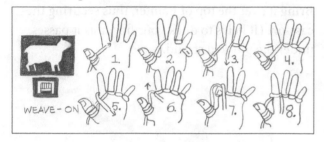

Rows

Lay the leed Pinkywise.

With your Shuttle bird-pinch, poke underneath the leed and pluck up the yarn-ring (the yarn loop on your finger) on Middler.

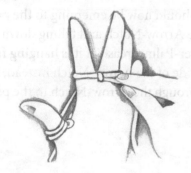

Give it a good tug toward yourself (elongating it, somewhat).

Lift the yarn-ring over the leed and over the top of that finger.

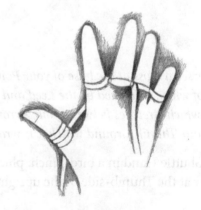

As you let go of the loop, you will see that it falls to the back side of Pointer, creating a stitch on the back side.

✳ This completes your first leaping-sheep stitch or *leapstitch* for short.

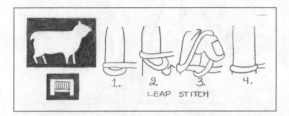

Complete the row by doing leapstitches on Ringa and Pinky. This completes the first outbound row of leapstitches.

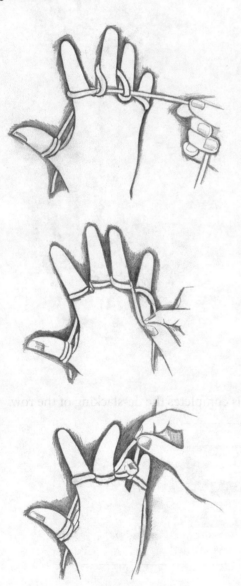

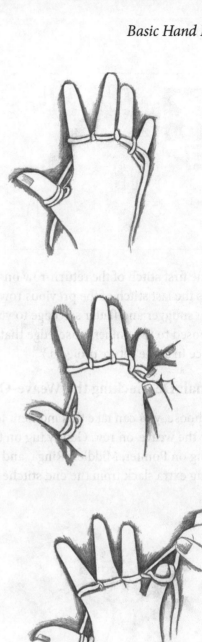

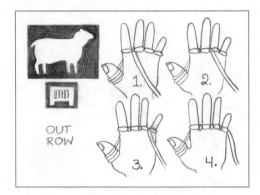

OUT
ROW

Begin the first stitch of the return-row on the same finger as the last stitch of the previous row. This creates a snugger and flatter selvedge to your work. (As opposed to the fluffier loose-edge that we will introduce in some future projects.)

Optional: De-Slacking the Weave-On Row

If you choose, you can take this moment to *de-slack* the weave-on row. Gently tug on the yarn-ring on Pointer, Middler, Ringa, and Pinky, removing extra slack from the end stitches.

✳ This completes the de-slacking of the row.

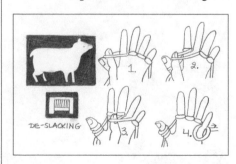

DE-SLACKING

Do your next row in the opposite direction (Thumbwise) on the same hand, as follows:

Lay the yarn up Thumbwise across the Palm, letting it hang down the back, and do a leapstitch on Pinky.

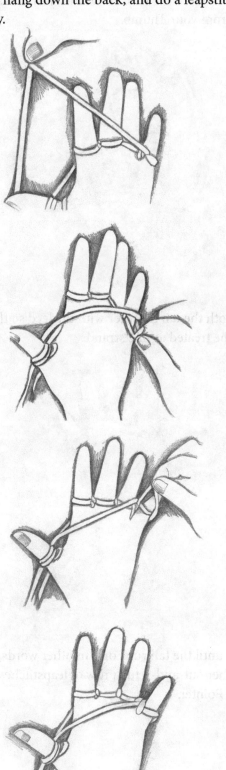

✳ This completes the Thumbwise leapstitch.

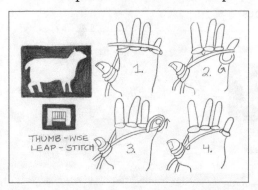

Do leapstitches on Ringa, Middler, and Pointer, in that order.

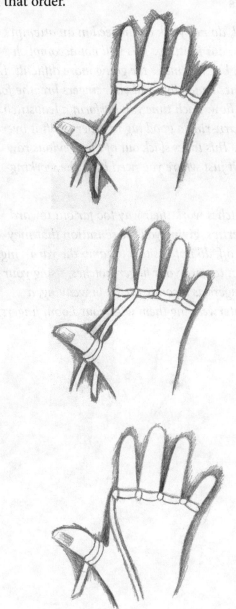

✳ This completes the out-and-return row of leapstitches.

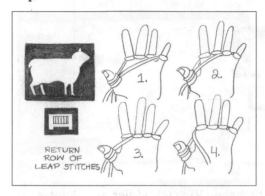

RETURN ROW OF LEAP STITCHES

1. 2. 3. 4.

Tensions

In general, do not yank on the leed in an attempt to tighten your knitting. This will not accomplish your goal, but will make the going more difficult. Let your stitches be flexible and your fingers breathe for a smooth flow. Each time you perform a leapstitch, give the yarn-ring a good tug in order to lift it over the finger. This takes slack out of the previous row and puts it just where you need it, in the working-row.

If your stitches work their way too far out toward your fingertips, giving you the sensation that they could fall off, do not hesitate to tamp the yarn-rings back down toward your finger-notches, using your Shuttle fingers as a comb, (or, as in weaving, a "reed,") interweaving them with your Loom fingers.

Optional Tail-Join

Continue knitting rows. You also have the option of working the tail into the fabric as you knit to have it out of the way. To do this, just unwind the tail from your Thumb.

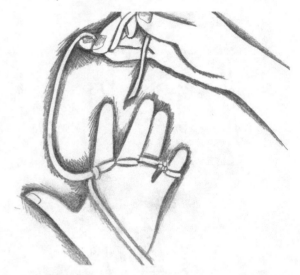

Smooth the tail together with the leed so that they will be treated as one strand.

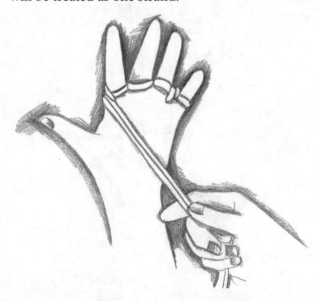

Knit until the tail runs out. In other words, do another out-and-return row of leapstitches starting with Pointer.

Notice that you will be leaping a single-strand over a double-strand. You may be temporarily confused to see that you are now plucking a double strand to make the leaps—but never mind, you are incorporating the end-strand into the work until it is used up. Then you will be back to leaping with single strands. (leed + tail).

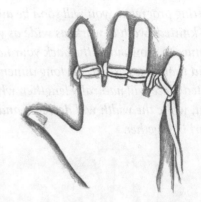

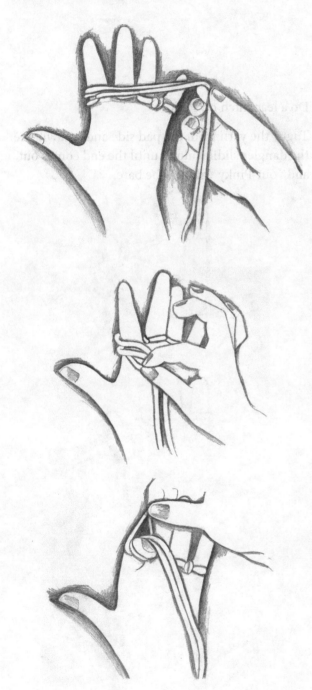

This action of smoothing the tail into the leed to hide it in the work is called a tail-join.

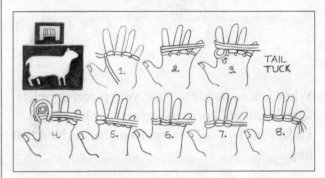

Continue doing rows of leapstitches.

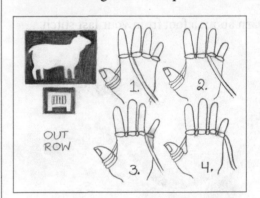

As your knitting progresses, you will soon be aware that a loose-knitted swath of work, as wide as your hand, continues to grow out of the back your hand. Keep in mind that once cast off, the long dimension of your knitted piece will naturally lengthen when stretched out, while the width will decrease and its sides will curl in together.

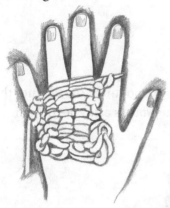

When you are ready to finish your piece, complete a final outbound row, ending on your Loom-Pinky. The leed will emerge from the stitch on that finger.

Secure-Off

Cut the yarn about a foot from your last stitch.

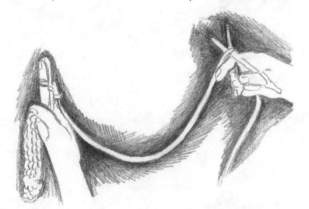

Remember to tuck-in the loose end of your yarn-ball.

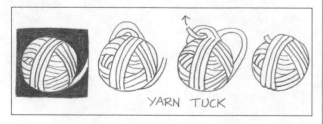

YARN TUCK

Lay the dangler Thumbwise up across your Palm, as you would for a normal return-row.

Do a leapstitch on Pinky.

Tug at the yarn from the pad side and you will see the dangler sliding along until the end comes out, and your Pinky will now be bare.

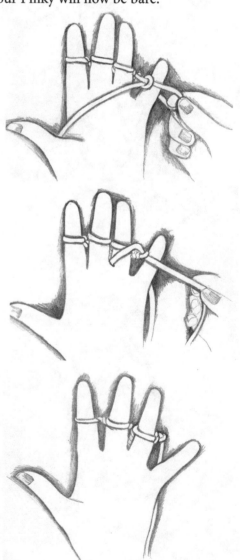

✳ This completes your first secure-off stitch.

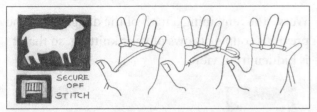

You may have noticed that the stitch that has fallen off is now secured against unraveling by the strand running through it. Your knitted rows will not be fully secure from unraveling, however, until the last stitch is secured and tied-off.

Next, lay the dangler across your palm again—it will be emerging from the bottom of Ringa—and do a leapstitch on Ringa. Pull the dangler through and out. Both Pinky and Ringa will now be bare.

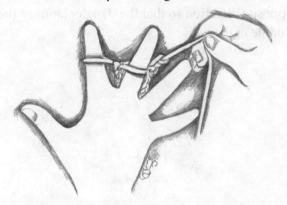

Repeat this process with Middler.

Now Pointer should be the only finger left with a yarn-ring on it.

Tie-Off

Take hold of a segment of the dangler and tuck a little loop of it down under the remaining yarn-ring on Pointer. Push the dangler through that loop.

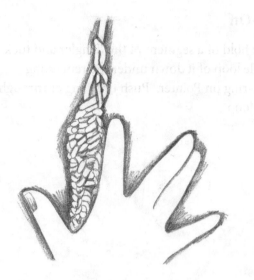

Release the final loop from Pointer and tug until snug, easing the resulting knot down against your work, as best you can.

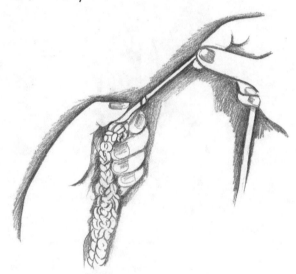

* This completes the basic tie-off.

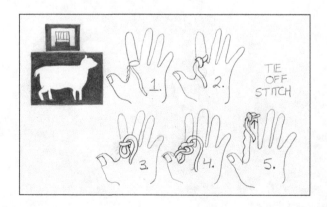

Weave-In

Weave the remaining length of the dangler into the previous couple of rows of your knitting, so that it is hidden from view.

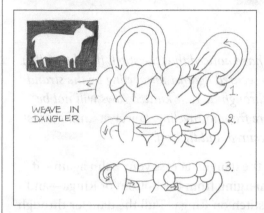

You may want to weave it back again in the opposite direction so that the dangler lands in the middle of the work.

Take your finished work in hand and tug at it firmly in all directions to even-out the tension and discover its completed form. Your journey with Bare Hand Knitting has just begun. In the projects section of this chapter, you will find a variety of projects for knitting on one hand.

Simple one-hand pieces, although limited in scope, can be very useful for making narrow scarves, head-ties, belts, and the like. Children, I have found, are delighted with even these simple creations. It is a foundation-stone for all of the other amazing techniques that you will learn in this book. Think of it as learning the scales on a musical instrument: very basic, but essential for future music-making.

Starting and Stopping

There will be times, of course, when you have to interrupt your knitting mid-process. On those occasions, in order to keep your place and keep the work from unraveling, you will need some kind of "stopper" to take the place of your fingers. For a very temporary place-holder, the stopper could be some kind of stick, like a pencil or chopstick. When you set it down, be careful to nest the project down into the bottom of your basket or other secure place, so the pencil will not slide out. For longer breaks from knitting, the work can be better secured with a tie.

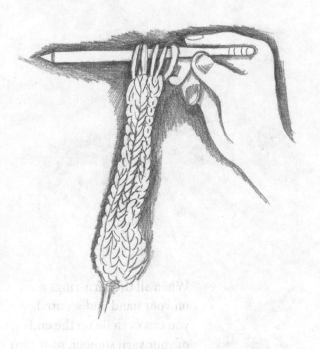

Yarn Stopper

Knit up a piece of chain-stitch, about 10 inches long, including the two tails. Weave the chain through the four stitches on the fingers and slip the stitches off after each one has the chain threaded through it.

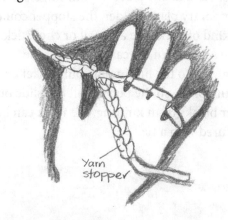

When all the yarn-rings are off your hand and secured, you can even tie up the ends of your yarn stopper, so it can't slip loose.

Quick Tie-Off Option

Another way to secure your yarn is to make the leed itself into a yarn stopper, as follows:

Draw out some slack with the leed, about a two-foot length and fold it back over on itself, to form about a 12-inch length of doubled-over leed, with a bight.

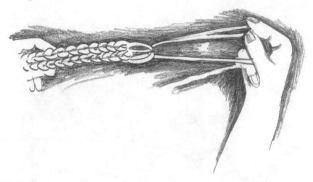

Bring the remaining double-leed around and tie it off on itself with a bowknot.

Ripple Stitches & Cornfield Stitches

Your knitted pieces have a top-side and a bottom-side. The pattern of small rounded bulges that appears on the upper-sides of each knitted piece resembles moonlit ripples on water. That is the ripple-side. The patterns of V-shaped lines that appear on the underside of the piece resemble a plowed field with young plants sprouting. This is the cornfield-side.

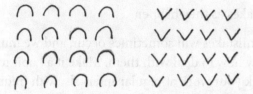

When a beginner to Bare Hand Knitting sets aside an unfinished piece and later picks it up again, she is liable to place it back on the hand upside-down and continue knitting. In that case, there will appear a peculiar rift in the pattern of the knitted piece.

This happens when the knitting is placed with the ripple-side facing downward instead of upwards. Once this mistake has been caught, remove the yarn-rings from your fingers and tug at the work-side of the leed to take out the recent rows.

Alternate

Another option is to adjust your pattern to include the change. Purposely including an alternation of ripple and cornfield patterns can enhance a design. If you go with this option, you will have to be mindful to continue flipping your knitting over, at regular intervals, to produce the desired design. Keep in mind, too, that whenever the knitted piece

is flipped over, the direction of the curling-in along the sides of the piece will also alternate.

As you progress through more advanced knitting techniques in Volume II, you will be introduced to more efficient ways of creating alternating patterns in wider pieces.

Fulling

Fulling is the act of washing a completed knitted piece by hand, with a bit of soap and warm water, to condition and strengthen it. This applies both to traditional needle-knitted fabrics and barehand pieces, alike. As with all wet-felting, the warm water relaxes the fibers and evens-out the tensions, smoothing the work and giving it a finished look.

In addition to applying a gentle hand-washing for this purpose, you can lay your knitted piece on a dish-towel and roll it up like a sushi, keeping it wet and soapy as you do so. Gently rock it back and forth. Do this several times, taking it out and rolling it from all directions for evenness. *Wet-felt rolling* brings a piece together in a nice way, shrinking it slightly. The technique is also used in wet-felting wool roving to form cloth, or *Nuno-felted* items.

The Rolling Method

The rolling method also comes in handy for consolidating the ends of your pieces. Starting and finishing rows on Basic Knit pieces are loose and a bit uneven-looking as compared to the body of the work. Once you learn the *leapfrog* technique introduced later in this chapter, this will no longer be the case. But for now, you can finish the end-rows by felting them down some. Just place the end-rows in a towel with a bit of soapy water and put some focused rolling action in this area so that the whole piece is not over-felted.

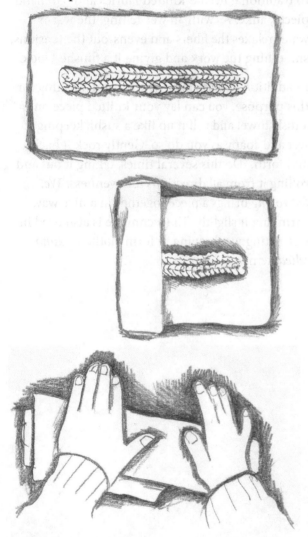

Finish with a rinse with cool water with a dash of vinegar and lay out your wet-fulled piece on a towel to dry; spread out in the shape you would like to encourage.

Fixing Mistakes

As is well known to needle-knitters, the only way to fix most knitting errors is to first undo your work all the way back to the mistake. Bare Hand Knitting is no exception. The saving grace for barehand knitters, is that fingers, unlike needles, have nerves, so that you are more likely to notice if a stitch is missed, or slips off the end of your finger, than if you are using an insensate tool. Also, the fact that your Loom Hand forms a sort of trellis, or frame that orders your work, allows you to catch mistakes as they happen.

But mistakes will sometimes occur, and we must know how to deal with them. Make it a habit to check your work at regular intervals, with frequent stops and checks.

A friend and fellow craftswoman who comes from an unbroken line of knitters on both sides of her family, says "Fixing mistakes is the best part of knitting, because, with knitting, we can go back and fix them."

When you first catch a mistake, stop knitting.

Un-Knitting

If the error lies a good number of rows back, then the best way to unravel the subsequent work is to first remove the work from your Loom Hand in the following way: remove the knitting from your fingers by gently pushing yarn-rings upwards till they all fall free of your fingers. Do not secure them. As you become used to doing this, you will find that it is easy.

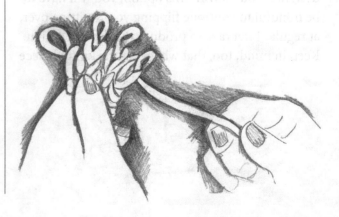

Tug gently at the leed until you have unraveled your work, back to a row or two before the mistake occurred, and fix it.

Replace each loop on the finger from which it was removed, same-side-up. (Another advantage to keeping your stitches not-too-tight is that replacing your stitches will go more smoothly.)

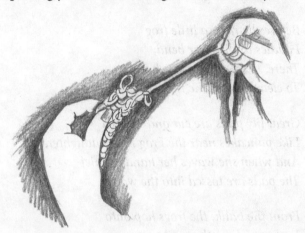

Now, with your work back on your Loom Hand, slowly undo stitches one-at-a-time, until you reach the mistake; fix it and then go forward, continuing to knit normally. (Carefully removing the last stitches with the work still on your hands, helps to retain the correct twist in your yarn-rings, so as to avoid creating a noticeable blemish in your work where you began knitting again.) Or, if the mistake in your knitting is not very far back (fewer than three rows), you may not need to remove the work from your fingers at all. In this case, simply work backwards, un-knitting, to remove one stitch at a time.

Dropped Stitches

If you "drop" a stitch, you do not necessarily have to take out your entire knitted piece back to that point. Needle-knitters are familiar with the technique of working the dropped stitch back up to the current row. First, remove the stitches from your fingers then replace them with the cornfield stitches facing up.

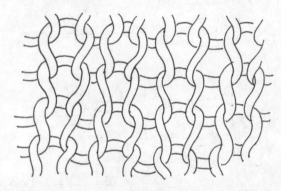

Next, scoot the loops aside in the fabric above the dropped stitch, creating an ascending series of horizontal "bars," like the rungs of a ladder, above the dropped stitch. Then, lay the empty loop above the first bar and draw a loop of that bar up through the empty loop, making a new loop. Continue upwards in this fashion until you reach the top row. There, the final loop is placed back on the proper finger.

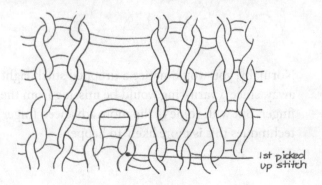

1st picked up stitch

Now remove the piece and flip it a second time so that the ripple stitches are facing up again.

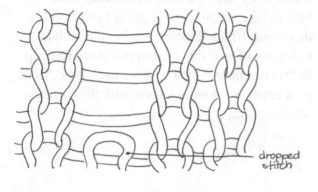

dropped stitch

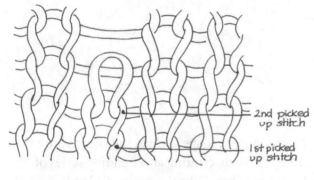

2nd picked up stitch

1st picked up stitch

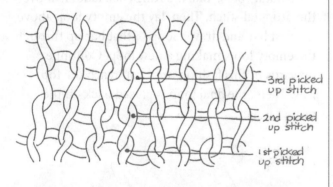

3rd picked up stitch

2nd picked up stitch

1st picked up stitch

Normally, you would notice a dropped stitch right away, since a yarn-ring would be missing from the finger. But with some of the more advanced finger techniques this is more likely to happen.

Leap-Frog Technique

The Froggies' Jamboree

Today's the Froggies' Jamboree,
With food and games, a River Race;
Tonight there will be music, dancing,
While fireflies light up the place.

Before the race, a little frog
Paddles to the river bend;
There, ties a ribbon to a bush
To clearly mark the race's end.

Great lily pads are cut and stacked
Like pancakes near the Frog King's daughter,
And when she waves her handkerchief
The pads are tossed into the water.

From the bank, the frogs hop onto
Empty pads as they sail past,
Then leapfrog closer to the middle
Where the current sweeps them fast.

As the lily pads pass under
A river-bridging fallen tree,
More frogs jump down and ride off swiftly—
They hop and spin and croak with glee.

Leapfrogging each from pad to pad,
The last is first, the first is last;
Along the banks the woodland creatures
Cheer the frogs as they sail past.

The first frog to reach the ribbon
Pulls it free and waves it high,
Shoots a long tongue in the air and,
Without trying, snags a fly!

Afterward, there is much feasting;
Dancing till the morning light,
With many a froggie-heart rejoicing:
"What fun to be a frog tonight!

– H. Akin

Now remove the piece and flip it a second time so that the ripple stitches are facing up again.

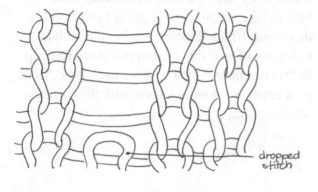

dropped stitch

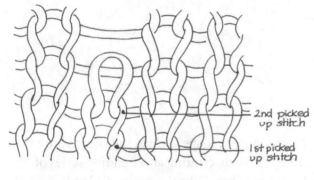

2nd picked up stitch

1st picked up stitch

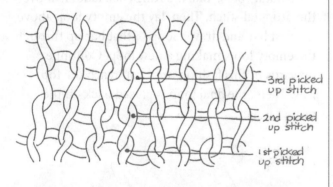

3rd picked up stitch

2nd picked up stitch

1st picked up stitch

Normally, you would notice a dropped stitch right away, since a yarn-ring would be missing from the finger. But with some of the more advanced finger techniques this is more likely to happen.

Leap-Frog Technique

The Froggies' Jamboree

Today's the Froggies' Jamboree,
With food and games, a River Race;
Tonight there will be music, dancing,
While fireflies light up the place.

Before the race, a little frog
Paddles to the river bend;
There, ties a ribbon to a bush
To clearly mark the race's end.

Great lily pads are cut and stacked
Like pancakes near the Frog King's daughter,
And when she waves her handkerchief
The pads are tossed into the water.

From the bank, the frogs hop onto
Empty pads as they sail past,
Then leapfrog closer to the middle
Where the current sweeps them fast.

As the lily pads pass under
A river-bridging fallen tree,
More frogs jump down and ride off swiftly—
They hop and spin and croak with glee.

Leapfrogging each from pad to pad,
The last is first, the first is last;
Along the banks the woodland creatures
Cheer the frogs as they sail past.

The first frog to reach the ribbon
Pulls it free and waves it high,
Shoots a long tongue in the air and,
Without trying, snags a fly!

Afterward, there is much feasting;
Dancing till the morning light,
With many a froggie-heart rejoicing:
"What fun to be a frog tonight!

– H. Akin

To create start and finish ends that are snugger and braid-like in appearance, the frog-stitch technique can be applied to any hand-knitted project in this book. The practice-project involves knitting several short pieces, in a row, so that you will have enough practice to get the hang of it. These small pieces will be gathered up as petals and used to make a flower.

Materials
To practice you will need five yards of yarn and a little tie, called a tell-tail, which is just an 8-inch length of yarn in a contrasting color.

Weave-on to the four fingers of your Loom Hand.

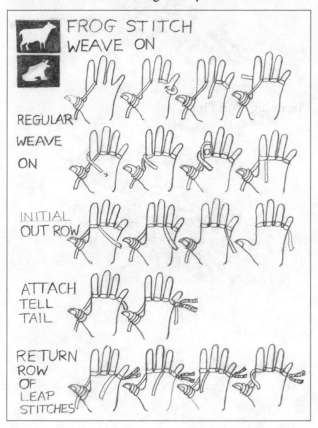

Do not de-slack your weave-on row nor do a tail-join, but rather, leave the tensions of your work as they naturally land, without tugging on the tail or the leed. At the end of the first out-row, attach a tell-tail tie to the leed, sliding it against Pinky.

Knit regular leap-rows as instructed earlier in this chapter and add one last out-row to end Pinkywise. (For the practice-project, knit 3 out-and-return rows, then add one last out-row to finish Pinkywise.)

Secure-off from Pinky, Ringa, Middler, and Pointer, keeping the tension of the cast-off stitches as they are. Do not tug on the leed or the dangler. Also, do not yet tie-off the last loop on Pointer.

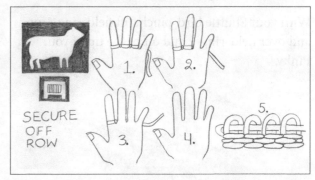

The work will have fallen from your hand now. Turn the knitted piece over so that the ripple-stitches are what you see.

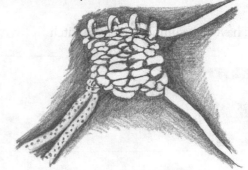

83

Secure-Off End

You will see four yarn-rings around the *standing part*, the length of yarn inside your work just before it emerges as the leed. Since you are viewing these rings just above the ripple side of the knitted piece, they will be called *ripple-rings* 1, 2, 3, and 4.

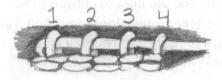

Carefully slip ripple-rings-1 and -2 onto your Loom Pinky. Your Pinky should lie inside the rings and just on top of the *standing part* of the yarn.

With your Shuttle bird-pinch, lift field-ring-1 up and over field-ring-2 and off of the tip of your Pinky.

✴ You have just completed a frog-stitch.

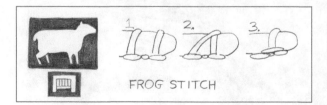

FROG STITCH

Frog-stitch ring-2, over 3, as follows:

Place ring-3 onto Loom Pinky next to ring-2.

With your Shuttle bird-pinch, lift ring-2 up and over field-ring-3 and off of the tip of Pinky.

Place ring-4 on Pinky.

With your Shuttle bird-pinch, lift ring-3 up and over ring-4 and off of the tip of Pinky.

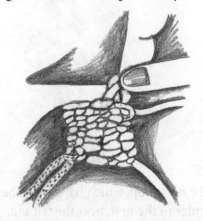

There should now be just one ring left on Loom Pinky, that being ring-4.

Tug gently on the dangler to remove any extra slack. Pull the tail through ring-4 to secure it off.

Gently snug-up the knot.

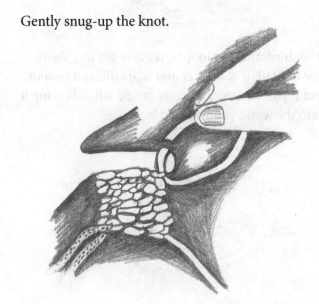

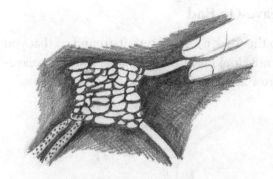

Here is a view of the finished end from the top.

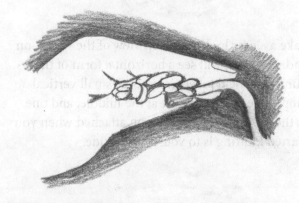

✳ You have now secured the frog-stitch row.

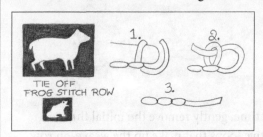

✳ You have now completed a row of frog-stitches on the finish-end.

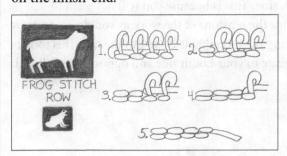

Weave-On End

Flip the work over and turn it around so that you are now looking at the field-side, with the weave-on row at the top end.

Take a closer look at the top view of the weave-on end. Here you will see a horizontal form of the number 8, held together by three small vertical loops: one at the top, one at the middle, and one at the bottom. The tell-tail you attached when you started knitting is to your Shuttle-side.

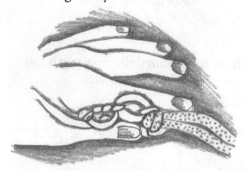

One at a time, gently remove the initial three consecutive loops that make up the weave-on row. To do this, gently tug at the tail-most side of each loop as you remove it, rather than tugging on the work side. This is because you will not want to change the tensions of the work as you do so. Start by tugging the loop that is closest to the tail. This loop is opposite to your Loom side and opposite the tell-tail.

Remove the next loop, which happens to be perpendicular to the first, near the tell-tail.

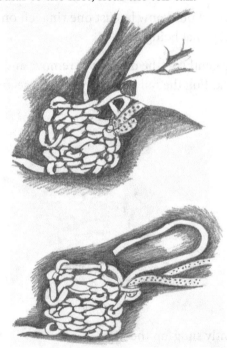

The third-and-last loop to remove sits just above the tell-tail. It is smaller and more difficult to spot, but if you tug ever so gently on the tail, following it into the work, you will find it.

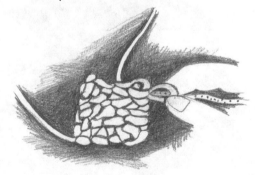

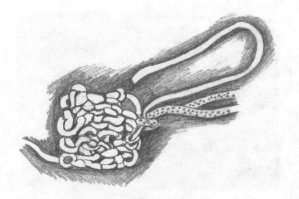

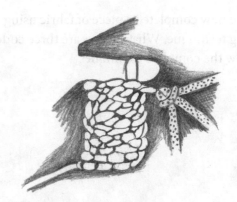

✳ You have completed the process of pulling loops out of the original weave-on row.

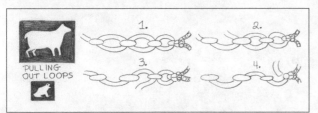

Straighten out the top-end a bit and you will see a row of four yarn-rings on a standing part, similar to the one you had seen on the secure-off end, only the fourth one has the tell-tail still attached. They are referred to as rings 1, 2, 3, and 4 on the ripple side.

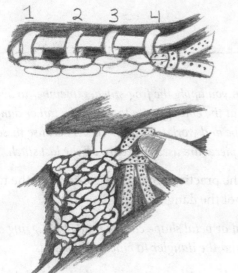

Place ring-1 and ring-2 on Pinky. Frog-stitch ring-1 over ring-2 and then ring-2 over ring-3. Now leap ring-3 over ring-4. At any time now, you may remove the tell-tail from ring-4. Tug gently on the *tail* to remove any extra slack from the whole row.

(In advanced projects, where you will be joining multiple pieces into a larger assemblage, it can be helpful to leave the tell-tails in place for the time-being, working around them, for easier alignment later. The tell-tails are helpful in marking the weave-on rows.)

Secure-off ring-4 with the tail. Gently snug-up the knot.

✳ You have now completed a sequence for applying the leapfrog technique on a weave-on end.

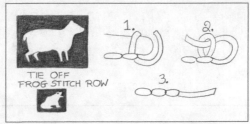

Your ripple side looks like this:

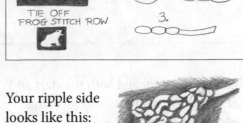

Your field side looks like this:

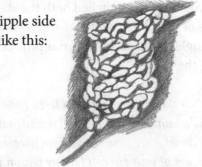

87

You have now completed a piece of fabric using the leap-frog technique. What follows are three codes that show the complete technique:

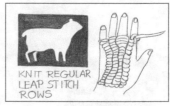

KNIT REGULAR
LEAP STITCH
ROWS

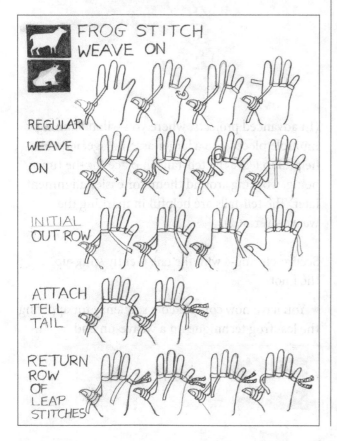

FROG STITCH
WEAVE ON

REGULAR
WEAVE
ON

INITIAL
OUT ROW

ATTACH
TELL
TAIL

RETURN
ROW
OF
LEAP
STITCHES

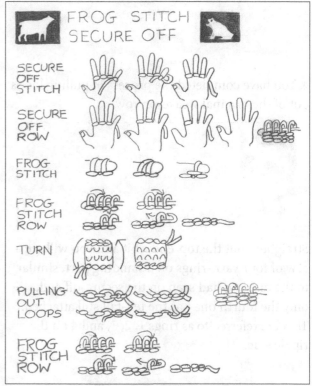

FROG STITCH
SECURE OFF

SECURE
OFF
STITCH

SECURE
OFF
ROW

FROG
STITCH

FROG
STITCH
ROW

TURN

PULLING
OUT
LOOPS

FROG
STITCH
ROW

Now that you have frog-stitched both the start and finish ends of your piece, you may weave-in the tail and dangler as usual, unless your project calls for leaving them out.

The field-stitch side is generally considered to be the upper side of a knitted piece. You will notice that the tail and the dangler are coming out from diagonally opposite corners of your piece. If for any reason you should ever want them on the same side, secure-off your knitting on an out-row, instead of on a return-row before frog-stitching the ends.

When you apply the frog-stitch, remember to always start at the end opposite to where the tail or dangler may be and work toward it. This is because these stray yarn pieces are used to secure-off the last stitch.

For the practice project, weave-in all of the tails but not the danglers.

A leaf or petal shape can be made by tugging on the tail and the dangler to cinch-in the ends.

A good way to practice this technique is doing a project that uses a number of leaves and/or petals.

Chapter Review for "Basic Hand Knitting"

Terms

- casting-on
- weave
- rows
- yarn-ring
- polystitch
- practice swatch
- outbound-row
- return-row
- selvedge
- un-knitting
- ripple stitches
- cornfield stitches
- dropped stitches

Operations

Palm-Heart Position

Place your open Loom Hand on your heart.
Bring your Loom Hand away from you by about a foot, remaining at heart level.

Tail-Join

Smooth the tail into the leed for a 2-ply strand.
Continue to knit with the 2-ply leed as if it were one, until the tail is gone.

Notable Elements

Lay the Leed Flow-Wise

Lay the working yarn in the direction that the work is currently progressing in.

Stitches

Leapstitch

Lay the leed flow-wise.
Reach under the leed and pluck up the yarn-ring.
Slip it over the leed and up over top of the active digit.

Rows Sequence

Outbound Row
On Loom Hand, lay leed Pinkywise.
Leapstitch on Pointer.
Leapstitch on Middler.
Leapstitch on Ringa.
Leapstitch on Pinky.

Return Row
On Loom Hand, lay leed Thumbwise;
leapstitch on Pinky
Leapstitch on Ringa.
Leapstitch on Middler.
Leapstitch on Pointer.

Weave-On for the Leap-Frog Technique:
Weave-on.
Complete initial outbound row.
Attach tell-tail to leed, next to Loom Pinky.
Complete initial return-row.

Secure-Off for Leap-Frog Technique:
Secure-off Thumbwise, without tying-off.

Shuttlewise Frog-Stitch:
Moving Shuttlewise, insert Loom Pinky through two consecutive yarn-rings.
Lift Loom-most yarn-ring over the next yarn-ring over, Shuttlewise.

Frog-Stitch Secure-Off (finish-end) Edge
Place work field-stitches up.
Frog-stitch secure-off edge, Shuttlewise.
Tie-off final frog-stitch.
Even tensions.

Frog-Stitch Weave-On (start-end) Edge
Place ripple-side uppermost.
Remove initial three weave-on loops.
Frog-stitch weave-on edge, Shuttlewise.
Remove tell-tail and tie-off final loop.

The Leap-Frog Technique
Prepare panel with leapfrog weave-on.
Knit desired number of rows.
Secure-off, Thumbwise, without tying-off.
Place work with field-stitches uppermost.
Frog-stitch secure-off edge, Shuttlewise.
Turn work around so that ripple-stitches are
uppermost and weave-on end is on top.
Remove initial three weave-on loops.
Frog-stitch start-end edge, Shuttlewise.
Tie-off final loop.
Remove tell-tail when appropriate.

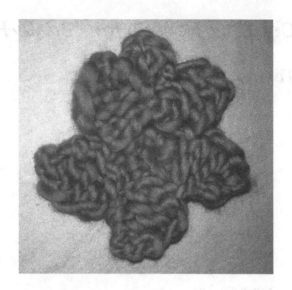

Projects for Basic Hand Knitting

Head or Waist Tie

Materials
¼ skein, 33 personal yards of Burly wool yarn

Steps
1. Weave-on to the four fingers of your Loom Hand.
2. De-slack the weave-on row and do a tail-tuck.
3. Knit 34 leap-rows.
4. Do the secure-off for your final row and tie-off.
5. Weave-in the tail and dangler.
6. Full the pieces and wet-felt sushi-roll the ends (optional).
7. Let dry
8. Measure around the crown of your head and tie-off with a square knot to secure it there.

Ponytail Tie

Materials
You will need 1/16 skein, 8½ personal yards of Burly wool yarn.

Steps
1. Do a frog weave-on.
2. Knit 12 leaping-sheep rows.
3. Do a frog secure-off.
4. Tie-off.
5. Weave-in tail and dangler.

Fluffy Boa

Materials
1 skein of any color of Worsted and Bulky 85% wool /15% Mohair with 100 8-inch strips of multi-colored Bulky yarn.

Steps
1. Attach 25 8-inch ties to leed using larks-head knots.
2. Weave-on with tail-end of leed.
3. Knit a return-row, keeping the ties out of the way.
4. De-slack the weave-on row.
5. Do a tail-tuck.
6. Begin to knit an out-row and, when you are half way, at Middler, slide a tie up to the Center Notch and push it through the Notch so that it is tucked under the work, then finish knitting the row.
7. Start knitting a return-row and slide a tie up to your Pinky Notch and tuck it through and under, then continue the row.
8. Knit an out-row, at the Arrow Notch, poke the ends through and under. Continue the row.
9. Knit a return-row, tucking tie through the Center Notch.
10. Continue knitting out-and-return rows, with one tie being poked through a Notch with each pass, and the Notches, starting with the Center Notch, following this pattern:
    Center, Pinky — Arrow, Center, Pinky — Arrow, Center, Pinky — Arrow, Center, Pinky…etc.
11. Repeat this entire pattern until your Boa is two personal yards long, attaching additional groups of ties onto the leed, as needed.
12. Secure-off and tie off.
13. Weave-in the dangler and tail.
14. Attach fringe to a single loop of each of the four stitches of the cast-on and cast-off rows.

15. Gently hand-wash your boa in some cool water with a few spoons of vinegar and let air dry.

16. Untwist each strand of fringe and gently separate into about three separate strands of fringe to fluff out the boa.

Chained Scarf

Materials
One skein of Medium wool yarn

Steps
1. Weave onto the four fingers of your Loom Hand using the frog weave-on.
2. Knit the whole ball of yarn (about 102 leap-rows).
3. Do the frog secure-off for your final row and tie-off.
4. Weave-in the dangler and the tail.

5. Form a slipknot from the knitted fabric about a foot in from one end of the scarf.
6. Starting at the slipknot, chain-knit the length of your pre-knitted strip, until about one foot from the end, as on p. 60, making a double-chain.
7. Poke the remaining end of your piece through the last big loop of chain and tug until snug.

chapter six
Alternating Yarn and Chain

Once you are practiced at finger-knitting and at *Basic Hand Knitting*, you can bring the two techniques together in a number of interesting ways. You may have already completed the project for chain-knitting a thick scarf, out of a hand-knitted panel; now find out what happens when you hand-knit a panel out of finger-knitted chain! Better yet, you can alternate between knitting regular yarn and chain knitted-yarn, bringing elasticity and variation into your projects.

Come Back Little 'Dillos

A fine little fez of three-banded armadillos
Snoozed the day through; downy roots are their
   pillows.
Come sundown, the "zed"—a girl pup—goes out,
Tracing termites and ants through her long, lowered
   snout.
The next one to leave is a boy pup—a "lister,"
Whose nose leads him straight away, after his sister.
When foraging leads the pups far from their home,
Only mother is left, digging roots up, alone.
But when her nose catches the scent of a puma,
She dives for her burrow, balling-up with a zooma!
Then, ever so slowly, peeking out through a crack,
She sees him, and seals off her shell with a clack!
Oh, when will her dear little 'dillos come back?

– A.B. Akin

Begin with a simple pattern that goes thin—wide—thin.

Add to your basket of tricks a smooth color-change technique called the felt-splice, and endless possibilities are at your fingertips.

You can *basic-hand-knit* your finger-knitted chain to create a stretchy piece. By alternating between regular yarn and chain-knit, you can create any number of neat projects, some of which are in the Projects section of this chapter. Follow these simple instructions to get your feet wet, before taking on larger challenges.

Creating a Stretchy Hairband

(This is a really neat project!)

Materials
One ball of Bulky yarn.

Prepare Yarn
For your practice-swatch, measure off 3 personal yards from the end of your ball of yarn and tie a slipknot at that point. This gives you a long tail that you will want to keep out of the way. An easy way to do this is to wind it into a mini hank: Take up the leed of your ball of yarn and hook the tail between your Loom Arrow-Notch, allowing about 6 inches of it to fall to the dorsal side.

Wind the yarn around the fingers (not the thumb) just as with the first step of rolling a ball of yarn. Wind all but one yard of the long tail.

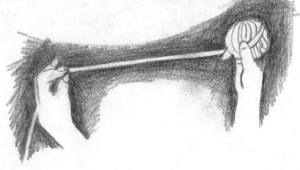

Slip this mini-hank from your fingers and secure it for the time by tying it off on the leed by its own tail, in a bow knot.

This little tied-up bundle of yarn can be thrown over your Loom side shoulder while you work, keeping it out of the way. (For larger projects of this kind this will be a more necessary step.)

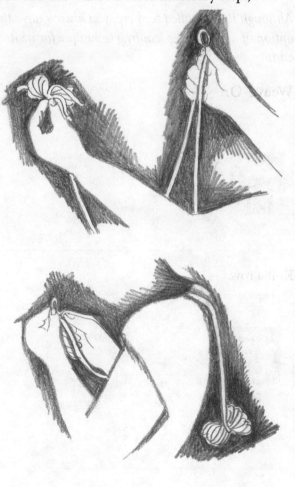

Taking up the slipknot you placed at the three-yard mark, begin chain-knitting the leed, in the direction away from the tail and toward the ball of yarn. Chain knit until you have 6 yards of knitted chain.

Open up the last slipknot loop of your chain and pop the whole ball of yarn through this hole, to secure-off the chain.

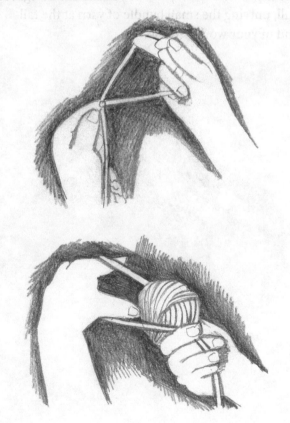

For your practice swatch, measure off another 3 yards from the end of your chain and cut the yarn off at that point. (*For larger projects you will want to attach a tell-tail to mark this spot, instead of cutting it, in case you will need to go back and adjust the length of your chain for the right measure. This is explained in the Projects section of this chapter.*)

Now for the fun part: you will just basic-knit the whole ball of yarn, according to the directions for basic-knitting.

Although it isn't called for here, you always have the option of applying the leapfrog technique for neater ends.

Weave-On

Beginning at the just-cut end, roll up the whole 12 yards of yarn—3 yards of yarn plus 6 yards of chain plus another 3 yards of yarn—into a single ball, untying the small bundle of yarn at the tail-end of your work to do so.

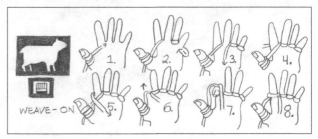

Knit a row.

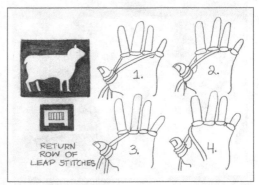

Do a tail-join.

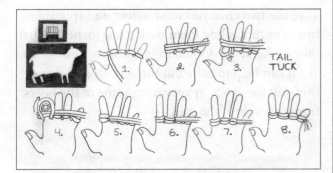

Do leap-rows until you reach the dangler, just around a 6-inch length for your end. In other words, knit the single strand of yarn right up to and through the knitted chain section. Continue until the chain is all used up and you have reached the single strand again. Keep on knitting until you reach the end, leaving a bit of dangler for weaving back in.

Slip the yarn-rings from your fingers and secure-off.

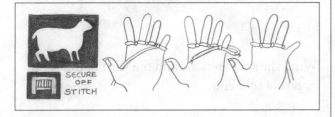

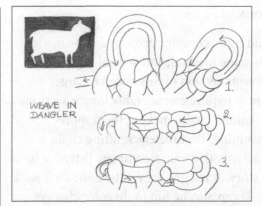

This will give you a band of knitted material that goes: narrow, wide, narrow. Stretch the band out by tugging at both ends to even tensions.

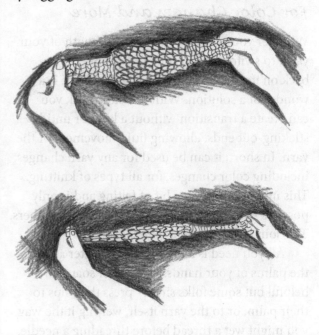

Tie the two skinny ends of your piece off on each other with a square knot. Your practice-swatch can be used as a doll-belt or a key-chain that can be worn on the wrist.

If you have chosen not to use the leapfrog technique for your start and finish ends, you can achieve similar tidy edges by *wet-felt sushi-rolling* the ends (chapter 5).

Variations

Larger and more complex projects can be made using this same method, and several are laid out in the Projects section of this chapter. Larger projects may require considerably longer sections of finger-knitted chain, making them more time-consuming. Fortunately, knitting chain is a calming activity that can accompany listening to music, a story or lesson, or even be done on a walk in nature. It can also be fun to do color changes with this technique.

The Felt-Splice
For Color Changes and More

Whether your goal is to extend the length of your yarn, to switch yarn colors, or to connect yarn back on itself to form a loop, the felt splice is a wonder of a solution. With this little trick you can create a transition without a knot or untidy sticking-out ends, allowing fluid movement of the yarn. In short, it can be used for any yarn changes, including color changes, for all types of knitting. This method involves a bit of felting and is only possible with yarns made from 100% animal fibers. This join is also called a *split-splice*.

All you need is a little splash of water and the palms of your hands. A touch of soap can be helpful but some folks simply press their lips to their palm, or to the yarn itself, wetting it the way you might wet a thread before threading a needle. This creates the right PH to aid in felting together the two ends. As is true for other felting methods, this technique will not work if the fibers which you are working with have been stripped of their natural scales through a "*superwash*," a chemical process used for bleaching yarns or rendering them "felt-resistant." This is rarely a problem unless your wool yarn is snow-white in color.

Instructions

Take the two ends you want to join and split the tips of each, pulling them back a few inches so that they look like the forked tongues of snakes.

It can help to tease out the split-tips a bit and thin-out the splice by removing some of the fibers from one side of the split.

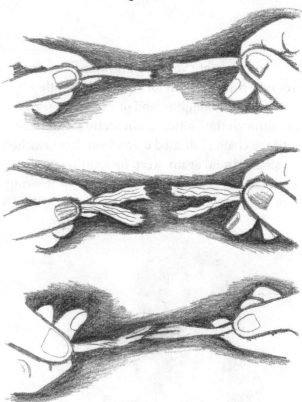

Slide the notches of the two splits together, so that they interlock and each overlaps the opposite strand.

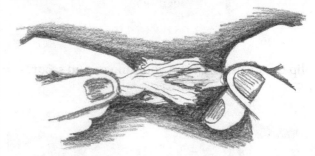

Wind the split ends around the yarn of the opposite split end.

98

Wet the palm of your Loom Hand and place the loose join there, ready for the next step.

Roll the loosely-connected strands vigorously back-and-forth between your palms until you can feel warmth created by the friction.

To test out your strand, allow the join to dry for a few moments then give the splice a little tug to make sure it holds.

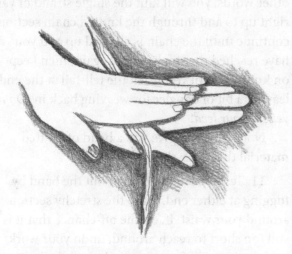

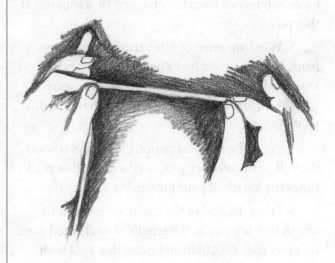

Check on your join, adding moisture as needed, and continue rolling the splice between your palms, slightly repositioning the yarn so that the whole length of the join receives some direct pressure and heat between your palms.

Continue wetting and rolling until the yarn is felted snugly into one continuous strand with no stray fibers sticking out—which should only take a few moments. If the yarn still appears lumpy in places, continue to rub until it is uniform throughout the length of the splice.

✳ You have now completed a felt splice.

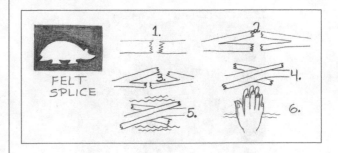

Projects for Alternating Yarn and Chain

Stretchy Waist-Tie

Be prepared that a fair amount of chain-knitting is needed, which does take time.

Materials

1 skein Medium wool yarn

Steps

1. Take a length of scrap yarn or string and measure around your waist, cutting it to size. Set it aside.

2. Take up your working-yarn and measure off 6 yards, 6 inches from the end, and tie a slipknot at that point.

3. Wind-up most of this yardage into a mini hank, securing it off by its own tail with a bow knot, and toss this little bundle back over your Loom-side shoulder to have it out of the way while you knit your chain.

4. From the initial slipknot, chain-knit toward the ball until you have produced a chain that is 13 times the length of your measuring string.

5. From the end of the chain, measure out a length that is equal to the length of unchained yarn that precedes the chain and mark that spot with a tell-tail. (We don't cut it yet, because we might need to make adjustments later.)

6. Secure the end of your length of chain by opening the final loop up big and popping the whole ball of yarn through it, tugging at the leed to snug-up the knot. That will lock the last stitch of the chain so it won't unravel.

7. Starting from the working-end, roll the yarn, including the chain-knit, back into a single ball, unloosing the hank at the end to do so.

8. Now comes the fun part! You will just *Basic-Knit* the whole ball, as follows: take up the tail and wind it around your Loom Thumb.

9. Weave-on.

10. Knit leaping-rows of simple four-finger knitting until you reach the end of the ball. In other words, you will knit the single strand of yarn right up to and through the knitted chain section, continue until the chain is all used up and you have reached the single strand again; then keep on knitting until you reach the tell-tail at the end, leaving a bit of dangler for weaving back in. *Do not yet cut your leed!*

Note: This will give you a band of knitted material that goes: skinny-fat-skinny.

11. Test the length: Stretch out the band by tugging at either end. Place the stretchy section around your waist. If, on the off-chance that it is still too short to reach around, undo your work back to the end of your chain, loosen the knot securing off your chain, and pop the ball back through to reopen the final slipknot. Add an additional length of knitted chain that is six times the length that you wish to add to your final piece, and take it from step-3 of this project again.

If, on the other hand, the stretchy part of the piece is too long, you will need to take out some of your chain to correct this.

12. Secure-off and tie-off.

13. Full the pieces, wet-felting, and sushi-rolling the ends.

14. Let dry.

Multi-Colored Bumpy Scarf

1. Measure and cut ten pieces of red yarn, each of them 10 personal yards in length.

2. Measure and cut nine pieces of green yarn of 4 personal yards each.

3. Take up one of your green lengths of yarn and felt-splice it to one of your red lengths of yarn.

4. Roll a ball beginning on the side of the green yarn, leaving a red loose end about a half-yard long, to work with.

5. Felt-splice a length of green yarn to the red loose-end coming from the ball.

6. Roll the ball again, leaving a half-yard of green loose-end to work with.

7. Continue this pattern of felt-splicing, alternating colors of your yarn-pieces together, rolling up your ball as you go.

8. When all of your yarn strands have been felt-spliced together, you should end with a green strand.

9. Now take up the green tail and begin rolling up the yarn in the opposite direction, beginning to form a new ball.

10. As you roll up the new ball, tie a slipknot a few inches **before** the first felt-splice/color-change (to red).

11. Using this slipknot as your first stitch, finger-knit a chain right through the felt splice, all through the length of red yarn to just a few inches **past** the next color change (back to green).

12. Pop the old ball of yarn (the one that is workwise and unwinding as you go) through the loop of the last slipknot of your knitted chain, securing that section of chain.

13. Return to rolling up your new ball, rolling it right through the red chain and the green yarn that comes after it, until you come near to your next color-change/felt splice.

14. Create a slipknot a few inches **before** the next color change (back to red), and finger-knit through the felt splice and the whole length of red

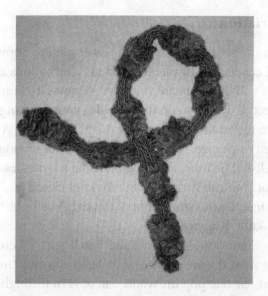

yarn and just through the next felt splice (color change back to green), popping the old ball of yarn through the last slipknot to secure-off this length of chain, as you did before.

15. Continue with this pattern: Rolling your new ball of yarn, creating a slipknot, chain-knitting through all the felt splices and all the sections of red yarn, securing your stretches of chain by popping the old and diminishing ball of yarn through the last slipknot of each chain, and rolling-up your new ball of yarn as you go, until all of your red sections have been transformed to chain.

16. Now you will *basic hand-knit* the whole ball of alternating yarn and chain to achieve a fat-and-skinny strip of knitted fabric. Here is a reminder of the steps:

17. Weave-on to your Loom Hand.

18. Knit an out-row.

19. De-slack your weave-on row.

20. Knit a return row.

21. Do a tail-join.

22. Knit in-rows and out-rows until your ball of alt-yarn-and-chain is all used up, leaving 12 inches to secure-off with.

23. Secure-off your last row.

24. Weave-in your dangler.

25. Wet-felt Sushi-roll the ends.

Variations

You do not need to follow the exact pattern above, but can vary your plain-and-chain alternations any way you like to create your own skinny-fat-skinny effect. One way to do this is to flag your working-yarn ahead of time, marking the points where you want to change, by tying a slipknot and inserting a tell-tail tie into each slipknot using a lark's head knot. You can then draw the slipknot closed against the tie (snug, but not too tight) without the slipknot disappearing.

Chain-knit between a pair of tell-tails, where you want the piece to be fat. When you reach the next tell-tail, pop the whole ball of yarn through the last slipknot of your chain, securing-off that section of chain. Then, remove the tell-tail, pull out its slipknot, and wind-up the whole length into a ball till you reach the following tell-tail. Remove it and start chain-knitting again. When all of the yarn has been prepared in this way, *Basic-Knit* the whole ball of yarn and, voila, you will have created a piece with alternating skinny-fat skinny sections.

If you do not wish to plan-out your exact pattern in advance but would rather add patches of chain spontaneously as you knit, you can stop knitting at any point, tie a slipknot in your leed and chain-knit a section of the leed, with the yarn-rings still attached to your fingers.

Either way you do it, you will need to remember to pop the whole ball of yarn through the last slipknot of your chain to secure it off before resuming with knitting rows. Many fun and interesting pieces can be created with this technique.

Measuring Tips for Your Own Projects

For each new project you will need to start by making a measuring-string. Use a scrap piece of string or yarn to measure out the length you want for your knitted section. Keep in mind that, as with the projects above, the chain itself requires three times as much plain yarn as the desired length of the final chain, and then you will need to produce a chain that is thirteen times the length of your measuring-string in order to achieve the same length in a *Basic Hand-Knitted* piece made from your chain.

To see if you have enough yarn for your project, do the following: Mark your measuring-string with a tell-tail—or a simple overhand knot tied onto a tell-tail, so it won't slide—at a point that represents the proportion of plain yarn to chain in your design. For example, if the sum of all the plain lengths takes up 2/3 of your measuring-yarn, with the rest is chain, then fasten the tell-tail 2/3 of the length from the beginning. Now take up another piece of string, as an intermediate measure and, holding the end in place with your finger next to the end of your first measuring-string, lay the strands parallel to each other until you get to the tell-tail. At that point, reposition your finger on the two strands and, for the final length, lay the intermediate strand back and forth three times on top, and then mark with a tie or cut.

Now, stretch out your intermediate measure and, with your ball of final working yarn, unroll back and forth 13 lengths-worth from the ball. That is how much you will need. This system works out well for Medium yarn, but may need to be adjusted for other thicknesses. The outcome will also depend on how tight your stitches are. Experience will be the best teacher in this, but just remember that it is better to start with extra yarn than not enough.

chapter seven

Whip-Stitching

Basic Whip-Stitching

The sizes of the barehand creations are not limited to the width of the hands. You will learn how to take a long skinny panel and bend it to join the edges, resulting in a wider piece. Whip-stitching is a simple and commonly-used stitch that involves sewing the thread around and around through the fabric in a way that traces out a coil through space.

The barehand method, although it can be accomplished with a large needle, does not require the use of any tools. You will be running a strand of yarn with a knotted tip—easier to tug on through the paired-up selvedge stitches along the sides of the knitted fabric.

Before getting started, it is important to show a key for all the different types of stitching yarns, ties, and various types of loops, as well as the danglers and tails. These threads, ties and loops are introduced at various sections throughout the chapter.

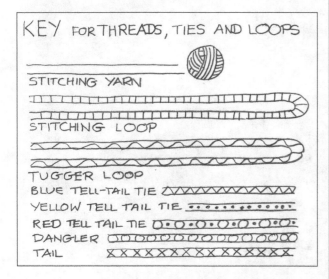

Create a Whip-Stitched Crown

Materials

- A ball of Burly yarn.
- 10 yards of stitching yarn in a contrasting color for the seam and the tie (the stitching yarn can remain attached to a ball of yarn as you work).
- Hand-knit a panel of fabric using the leapfrog technique.

Instructions

Do the frog weave-on sequence.

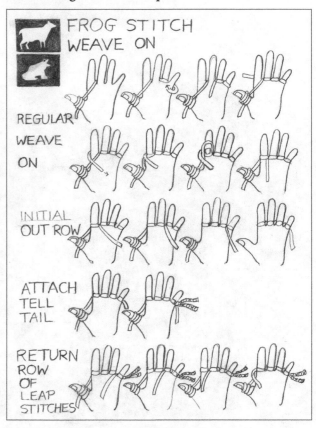

Knit leap-stitch rows—about 80 regular rows—to a length that will fit around the head of the wearer twice, at a slight stretch. It will be preferable to have it a bit on the shorter side, rather than the longer, because the knitting is stretchy and will be secured to the head with an adjustable tie.

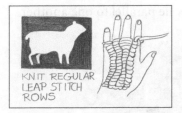

Do the frog-stitch secure-off sequence:

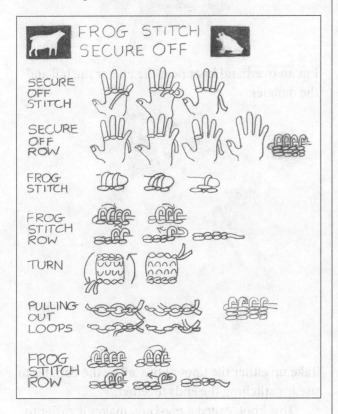

Condition Selvedge
Fishtails and Fish-lips

This is an excerpt from a gnome's journey later on in the chapter.

The fishes, as they bobbed along
Slapped their tails and sang a song.

Once you have completed your knitted panel, stretch out the selvedges to condition them for stitching.

Now, examine the conditioned selvedge: stretch out a section between your hands and you will observe a chain of stitches that can be said to look like alternating fish-lips and fishtails. The fish-lips appear as two parallel lines and the fishtails are the shorter linking-stitches in-between. Learning to differentiate between the two is important both for attaining proper alignment and to help you count rows. Whereas counting single rows by the rungs becomes tricky, once you have stretched out your work, you can easily count out-and-return rows by counting the fish-lips—skipping fishtails—along the selvedge.

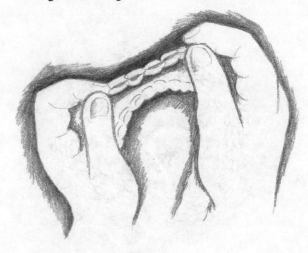

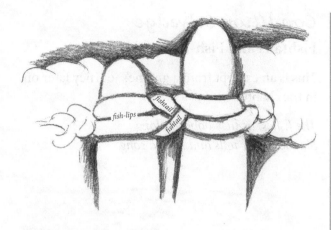

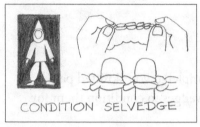

CONDITION SELVEDGE

Finishing the Ends

Next, examine the ends of your work. Each of the four frog-stitches, on either end, has a heart-shaped look to it. Now there are four pairs of parallel frog-stitches on each end. To begin with, you will stitch the ends together.

Gently tug on the tail to remove any extra slack from your stitching but be careful not to draw the tension any tighter than the rest of the knitting. Do the same to the dangler.

Lay out the knitted strip in a flat ring.

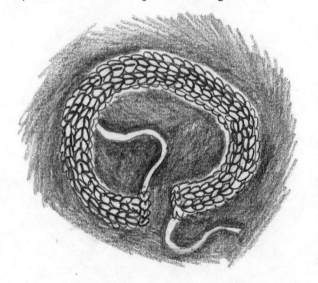

The leapfrog rows now lie parallel to one another.

Put an overhand knot near the end of the tail and the dangler.

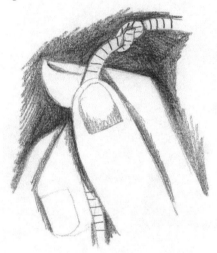

Take up either the knot of the tail or the dangler to use for stitching the ends together.

This knot, called a *tug-knot*, makes it easier to grip the yarn as you pull it though.

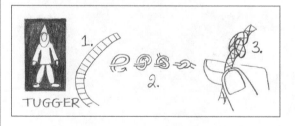

TUGGER

Push the knot through the heart-shaped frog stitch on the opposite edge.

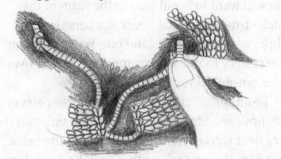

Continue weaving the strand of yarn in and out through each parallel pair of frog-stitches.

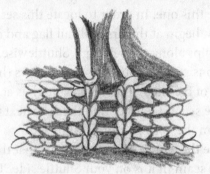

Gently pull on the tug-knot to draw the *start* and *end* rows together, so the two ends connect. Tug gently at the yarn and tug at the connecting seam until the tensions are worked out and the seam is snug and even.

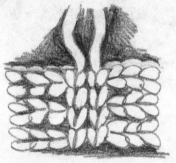

You have stitched together the start-end and finish-end of your knitted panel.

Hide the Ends

To secure the work and hide the ends, weave the tail under a few yarn rungs on the ripple side of the work, toward the middle of the knitted fabric.

Cut the tug-knot, leaving 1½ inches outside of the fabric.

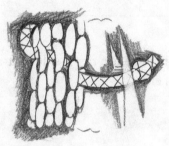

Split the tail.

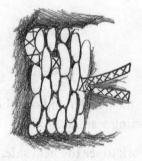

Push one side of the split under the nearest ripple stitch.

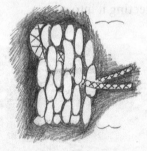

Using a square knot, tie the two split ends together, fastening the tail to a yarn rung.

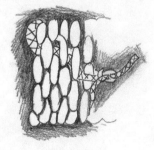

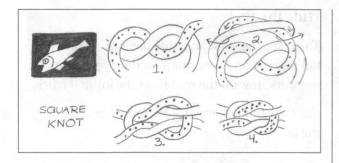

* You have now done a ripple side split-and-fasten to both yarn ends.

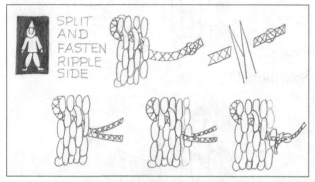

Do the same with the dangler, only on the other side of the connecting seam.

Turn over your work to see the field side, it will look a bit different on the upper side.

The strip of knitted fabric is now stitched together, end to end, connecting it into a loop.

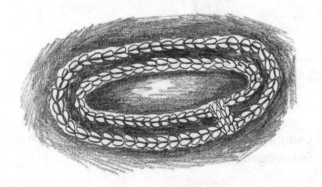

Flag the Bends

You will want to avoid having the seam of the stitched-together ends occur at a bend in the fabric, where it would stand out. For this reason, it is necessary to move the center of the work over by three out-and-return rows, as follows:

From the stitched seam, count three pairs of fish-lips over, Shuttlewise. Place a tell-tail, into the very next stitch over, Shuttlewise, into the fishtail. This flags the spot where there will be a bend in the work.

The second tell-tail will flag the bend that is opposite this one. In order to locate this seam with accuracy, begin at the first tell-tail flag and count the fish-lips along the selvedge, Shuttlewise. If your fabric consists of 40 out-and-return rows (having 40 pairs of fish-lips), the halfway mark is at 20. Place the second tell-tail into the very next fishtail over from the 20th pair of fish-lips.

Place the work in front of you so that the side with the seam in it is on your Shuttle side. The 40 parallel sets of fish-lips should now be lined up in readiness for stitching together.

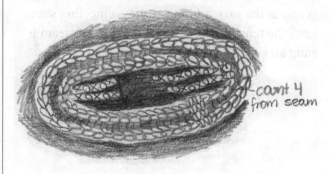

count 4 from seam

Stitching

Begin

Take up a leed of your ball of stitching-yarn and place a tug-knot close to the end.

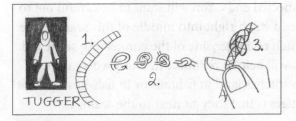

Begin stitching at the Loom side, as you will be stitching the seam Shuttlewise. In order to stretch the hole you will be stitching through, push your Shuttle Pointer down through the first set of parallel fish-lips—behind and through the two parallel pairs of fish-lips on either side of the tell-tail flag. (It is also possible to use your Loom Thumb to accomplish this.)

Use your Loom bird-pinch to push the tug-knot up, and feed it through the hole, against Shuttle Pointer.

Pluck up the tug-knot with Shuttle bird-pinch as it protrudes from the stitch, to pull it through.

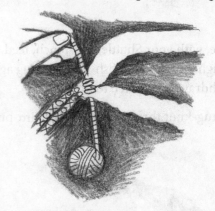

Hand off the tug-knot to your Shuttle bird-pinch and pull a personal-yard's length of stitching-yarn through, leaving the rest connected to the ball of yarn.

Bring the tug-knot back to the same side that the initial stitch was drawn through, only one set of fish-lips over.

As before, with your Shuttle bird-pinch, feed the tip through both pairs of fish-lips, pushing against your withdrawing Pointer, to do so.

Pull the tug-knot through with Loom bird-pinch.

Hand-off the tug-knot to your Shuttle bird-pinch and draw the strand all the way through.

✳ You have completed a whip-stitch.

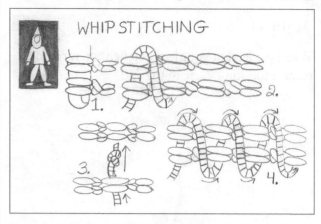

Continue to work whip-stitches along the seam and when you are three stitches away from completing the seam, you will have reached the connected ends. You will want to be careful not to place a stitch right into middle of this seam. Place a stitch on either side of the connecting seam and this will help to reinforce it. Don't worry if these two stitches land in fishtails or in fish-lips. All that matters is that they sit next to the seam.

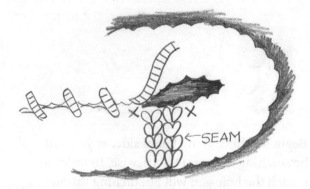

Continue to work whip-stitches through the remaining sets of fish-lips.

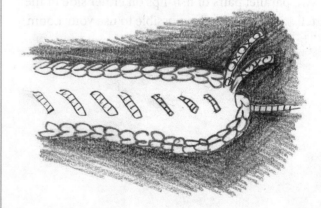

De-Slack the Seam

When and if you should need more length in your stitching-yarn, pull the extra slack through from the ball side, drawing the slack out one stitch at a time, until it has worked its way into the free stitching yarn.

Your stitches should not be too tight—causing a gather in the work—and not too loose, either, which could leave a slit between columns. And more importantly, your stitches should match one another. Fluid but controlled workwise movements for drawing-in the slack will work better than focusing on and comparing individual stitches.

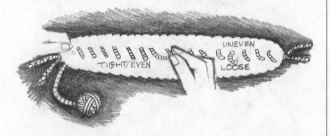

Bring the slack all the way through the seam of stitches, drawing it out into the leed.

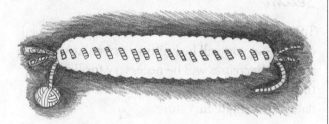

Adjust the tensions as necessary until you have accomplished relative uniformity of stitches.

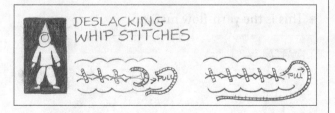

Weaving-In Ends

Once the seam is complete, cut the dangler and the tail at 8 inches. Tie a tug-knot onto the tail and the dangler.

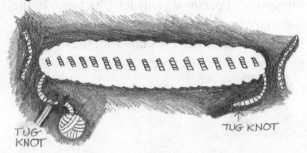

Weave the tail and dangler back in, each on its own side, along the seam you have just stitched.

Cut the tug-knot to remove it.

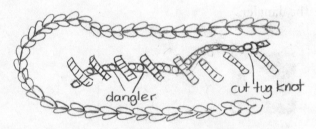

Split and fasten the dangler along the seam.

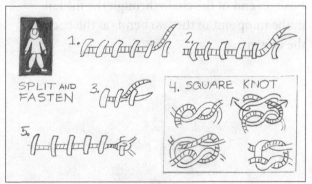

Do the same with the tail.

Making the Tie

You will need a tie with which to secure the crown to the head.

Finger-knit a personal yard's length of yarn in the same color as the stitching-yarn. Weave the tail into the work and do the same with the dangler.

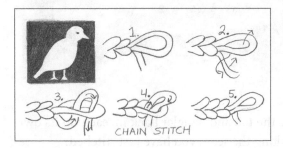

Weave the tail into the work and do the same with the dangler.

Push an end of the chain through the fishtail in the midpoint of the two bends at the back of the crown.

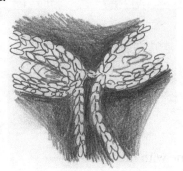

Use the finger-knitted chain for tying off the back of the crown.

Fit the crown on the head and adjust the length of the tie as needed.

Whip-Stitching a Spiraling Seam

This method is similar to the one you just learned, except that you will be knitting a circular spiraling seam, so *increases* will be necessary for flattening the piece. The practice-project will be relatively flat, with a slight curvature.

Also, as was the case with the previous project, you don't need to cut the yarn; it can remain attached to the yarn-ball as you work.

* This is the yarn-flow method.

You will want yarn of the same thickness, or a little thicker, as that used for the knitting.

Create a Toadstool Top

Before or after you knit your top, find a small wooden stump of about the width of one hand to place your toadstool top on. It can be a nice project to remove the bark from a stump, sand it down and polish it, giving your project the real look of a toadstool.

Knit a length of fabric that is 110 rows long, using the leapfrog technique for the start-end and finish-end as was done for the crown.

When you cut the dangler at 8 inches, place an overhand knot in the tip of it to mark this as the *finish-end* of the knitted panel, differentiating it from the *start-end*.

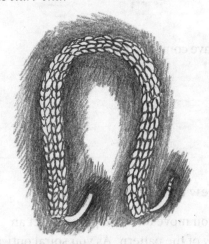

Do not weave-in the tail or the dangler.

Condition your fabric.

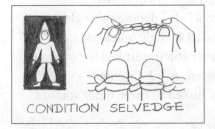

Count 6 fish-lips in from the start-end, working toward the finish-end: the end where you had placed a knot on the dangler. Attach a tell-tail right next to the sixth fish-lips, on the very next fishtail over, workwise, marking what will be a bend in the work.

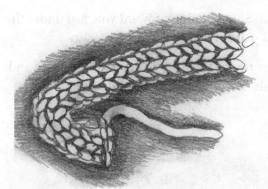

Count another six pairs of fish-lips over, workwise, from the attached tell-tail. To the very next fishtail you will now fasten the tail of the knitted panel. Do this by pushing a bight of the tail behind the fishtail and drawing the tip of the tail through this loop.

There is now a closed bend in the fabric.

Place the knitted fabric so that the loop with the tie is in front of you, and the bend with the tell-tail is to your Shuttle-side, and the corner side with the tied tail of the fabric is to your Loom-side.

Take up the loose end of your stitching-yarn and place a tug-knot into it.

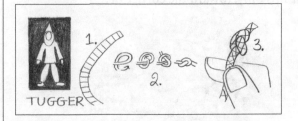

Stretch the loop, closing it, so that the inner selvedges lie parallel, against each other. This is the seam that you will be stitching together. You will begin by stitching together the first parallel pairs of fish-lips from the tell-tail tie at the inner fold of the loop.

Push Shuttle Pointer toward you, just under the two pairs of fish-lips to open the way.

Take up the tug-knot in your Shuttle Hand and begin sewing a seam of whip-stitches.

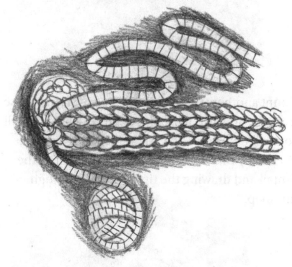

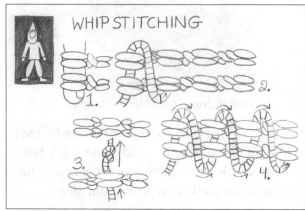

Continue to whip-stitch through parallel sets of fish-lips only, toward the corner tie.

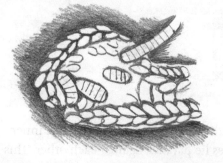

At this junction you will be stitching into the start-end of your work where the frog-stitches will look and feel a little different and there are no obvious fish-lips or fishtails.

Work three more whip-stitches connecting the selvedge to the frog-stitches along the start-end.

When you have worked up to the next stitch, you will accommodate the upcoming bend in the work by increasing the number of stitches along the inner selvedge of the spiral. To do this, stitch the next set of parallel fish-lips together and bring the stitching-strand into the next pair of fish-lips over along the outer selvedge of the spiral, but into the same pair of fish-lips along the inner selvedge of the spiral.

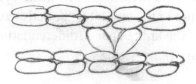

＊ You have completed an increase.

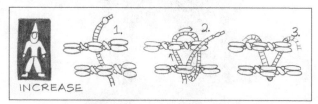

Overview of Spiral Pattern

Before you move forward, pause to get an overview of the pattern. As you spiral outward, it is necessary to regularly link one stitch on its inner row into two stitches in the corresponding outer row, according to the following pattern:

In this pattern a "-1-" denotes a single inner stitch being linked to a single outer stitch. A "-2-" means a single inner stitch is linked to two outer stitches, as illustrated. A "-3-" denotes a single inner stitch being linked to three outer stitches.

-1--1--1--1--1--1, -2--2--2--2--2--2, 1--2--1--2--1--2--1--2--1--2--1--2

For this project you will end with the following pattern just to bring your spiral to a closing point.

-1--1--2--1--1--2, -1--1--1--3-

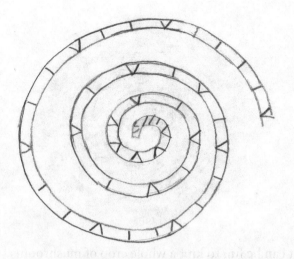

If you decide to expand upon this pattern, continue to whip-stitch your spiraling seams, working six evenly distributed increases along the outer selvedge, for every spiral. It follows that you can also decrease the circumference of a spiraling row by ceasing to add any increases as you stitch the next seam.

Continue Whip-Stitching

You have already stitched the first spiraling row, with single whip-stitches.

Stitch the second spiral: increase, increase, increase, increase, increase, increase into the inner spiraling row, in accordance with the numbered pattern given above.

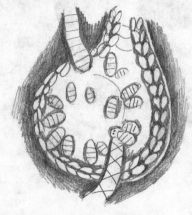

The inner fish-lips will each have two wraps of stitching-yarn passing through them, and the outer fish-lips will each have one wrap of stitching yarn through them.

For the next spiral, do: single-stitch, increase—single-stitch, increase—single-stitch, increase—single-stitch, increase—single-stitch, increase—single-stitch, increase—in accordance to the numbered pattern given above.

Bring the desired toadstool shape to your piece, by finishing with: single-stitch, single-stitch, increase, in accordance with the numbered pattern given above.

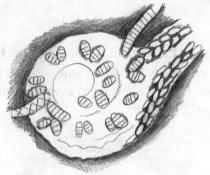

De-slack the seam before ending the pattern.

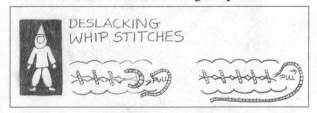

DESLACKING WHIP STITCHES

Finish by working the three frog-stitches of the end-row into one fish-lips stitch on the inner selvedge (a double increase), completing the numbered pattern given above.

115

Cut both sides of the stitching-yarn at about 8 inches and weave each back under its seam, doing a split-and-fasten to each.

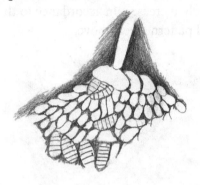

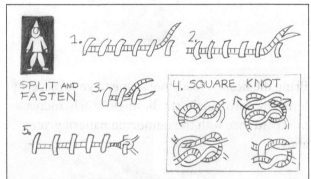

Also remove the lark's head knot from the tail of the piece and weave it in. Gently stretch your toadstool in every direction to even the tensions of your work.

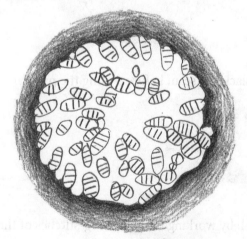

Turn your work over—field stitches uppermost—to view the good side of your finished piece.

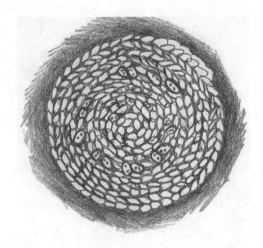

It can be fun to knit a whole crop of mushrooms in different colors to decorate a classroom or play area!

Create a Multicolored Gnome Rug

Materials

You will want Bulky-sized yarn in a variety of colors to knit with. This is a great project for using up your yarn scraps. To achieve a combined length for making the practice project you will want 30 personal yards. The color changes introduce an artistic element into the piece.

Color Changes

Prepare a multi-colored ball of yarn by fastening each of your yarn scraps together end-to-end.

There are various ways of joining yarn pieces for color changes, such as the felt-splice described in chapter 6. For this practice project, connect your strands using a two-strand overhand knot.

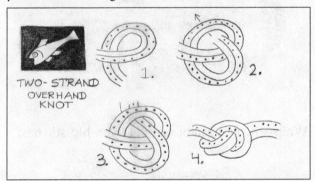

For this project, knots and ends don't matter. The ends can just be tucked into the back side of the work (the ripple side), where they tend to fall, anyway, to have them out of sight.

You will have enough when the multi-colored ball of yarn is about thirty yards long.

Stitching-Yarn

You will be using the yarn-flow method to stitch the rug, so there is no need to cut the stitching-yarn from a ball.

To whip-stitch any seam, you will need a length of yarn that is at least two-and-a-half times the length of that seam. For a pleasing decorative effect, use a stitching-yarn of a contrasting color in a lighter shade.

You will also need to prepare one tell-tail tie of 8 inches in length.

The knots, and ends that stick out from the knots, will naturally float to the ripple side of the work as you knit. This will become the backside of the finalized piece and won't show through. Any stray knots that might happen to fall the other way can be tucked out of sight later.

Knit Fabric

Using your multi-colored yarn, knit a length of hand-knitted fabric with frog-stitched ends 200 rows long. (Or 100 out-and-return rows.) Do not weave-in the tail or the dangler.

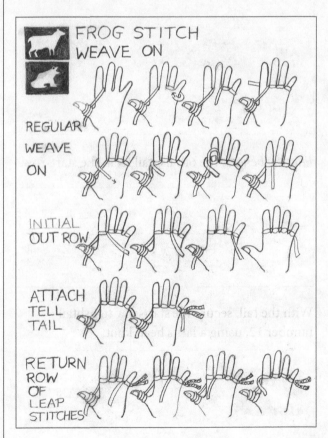

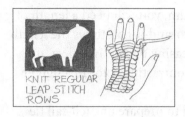

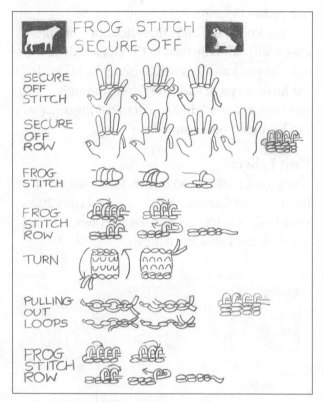

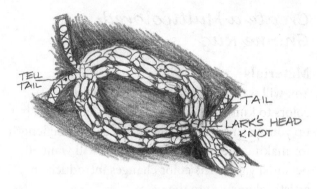

Place a tug-knot near the tip of your stitching-yarn, and begin whip-stitching at the flag on the 6th fishtail from the start-end.

Whip-stitch a straight seam of five whip-stitches.

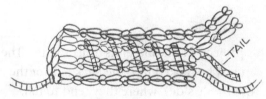

You will now work six increases to round your first bend, beginning with an increase into the fifth set of fish-lips—the one just before the tie at the corner of the start-end.

Stitch the selvedge to the start-end, increasing into each of the four heart-shaped leapfrog stitches along the start-end.

Finally, increase into the first fish-lips along the inner selvedge on the opposite side of the start-end.

✳ You have completed the six increases, to round the first spiraling row.

Flag the bend at the 6th fishtail from the start-row.

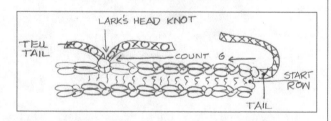

With the tail, secure the start-row to fishtail number 12, using a lark's head knot.

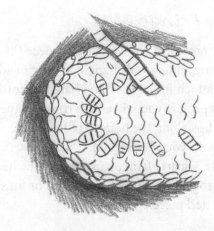

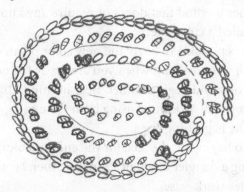

Increase by three into the last stitch of the inner selvedge.

As you work, pull through additional stitching-yarn, as needed.

Work two regular whip-stitches, and it is already time to start a set of six increases to round the next bend.

Continue whip-stitching in an oval by whip-stitching a straight seam between bends and placing six increases to round each bend, until you have reached the end of the knitted fabric.

Cut the stitching-yarn leaving an 8-inch end.

Weave-in the stitching-yarn together with the dangler, and split-and-fasten the end of each.

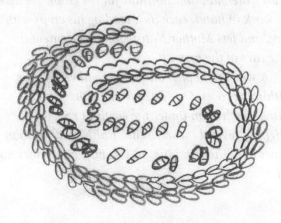

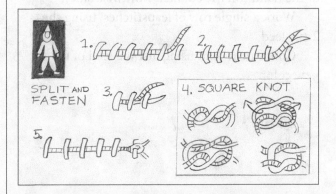

As you work, pull through additional stitching-yarn as needed.

De-slack your stitches and even the tensions.

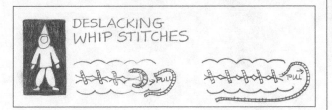

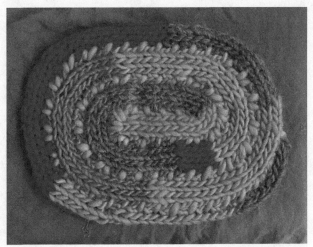

Color-Change Variation

In order to make color changes as you go, there is another method that does not require any knots at all, called a color-merge.

It is possible to begin the new color on an out-row or a return-row, when you are ready to end one color and begin another. Bear in mind, that one row will be knitted using both the ending-yarn and the beginning-yarn.

To begin, cut the leed for the ending-color, leaving a dangler of about 12 inches, then lay the dangler work-wise.

Drape the leed for the beginning-color across the hand, alongside the dangler of the ending-color, leaving a six-inch tail to drape over the side of the hand (on the counter-workwise side).

Work a single row of leapstitches, using the 2-ply leed.

Continue to knit using just the leed of the new color.

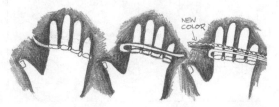

✳ You have completed a color-merge. (A color-merge can be implemented at any gap.)

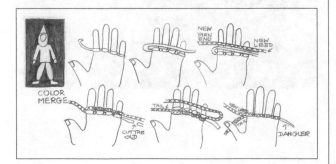

Adding Fringe

In order to transform an oval-shaped piece (like the gnome rug) into a wall-hanging, you can add fringe, and attach it to a stick and hanging-cord.

For this project you will attach fringe to the row of fish-lips along the bottom of the piece, beginning with your Loom side. (For some projects (like a scarf) fringe can also be attached to the row of frog stitches on the start-end or finish-end of a knitted piece.)

Farmer Anthony Plants His Crop

A hard-working farmer has prepared the soil and laid out the beds for a nice crop of fennel. He loosens the fertile soil, making little holes where he will sow the seeds. Dry straw is prepared and laid out in stacks. It will be used as cover for his rows, keeping them warm, protected and moist. The good farmer counts his blessings, thankful for the fertile soil, clean water, air, and sunshine for his crops. He takes his work in hand, each day, tending his crops with care, and lets Mother Nature and the elementals take care of the rest.

A wonderful phenomenon is gathering force within the roots. One fine day, a feathery plant pushes forth from under the earth. It reaches the height of several inches. With healthy roots it soon grows tall. The wind tugs at it gently, but it does not get uprooted.

Create a Fringed Wall Hanging

Choose colors you would like for a wall hanging and follow the steps for creating a gnome rug, above. You will now add fringe to it.

Determine which is the top and bottom of your wall hanging. There should be about 14 fish-lips stitches along the bottom selvedge.

Cut 14 pieces of yarn, each a half-a-yard in length: 7 in one color and 7 in another.

For a pleasing color scheme, you can have half of the pieces the same color as the stitching-yarn, and half a different color.

Take one cut-strand of each color, smooth them together into a pair with the ends lined-up. Repeat until all of the yarn strands are paired up.

Attaching Fringe

Widen a hole by poking through it with your finger.

Hook the middle of the pair of strands around Loom Pointer to fold it neatly in half, making sure the ends are of equal length. You have formed a bight in the pair of strands.

Feed the bight of the pair of strands up through the hole, pulling it through until it sticks up at least an inch.

Poke your Loom bird-pinch through the loop and pull the whole clump of four end-strands through it, forming a 2-ply lark's head knot.

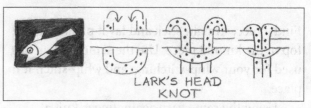

LARK'S HEAD KNOT

Tug gently on the strands to snug-up the knot.

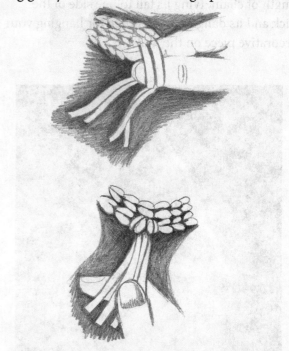

✻ You have now attached fringe to a stitch.

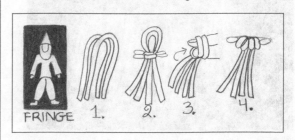

FRINGE   1.   2.   3.   4.

Do the same with each of the remaining pairs of strands until the row of fringe is completed.

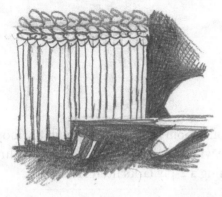

Find a nice, straight stick and lay it parallel to the top of the knitted piece. Use the same yarn as was used for your whip-stitching, and whip-stitch it in place.

Using the same yarn again, finger-knit a length of chain, tying its tail to one side of the stick and its dangler to the other, for hanging your decorative piece on the wall.

Patterned Whip-Stitching

Locating and securing proper alignment between sections of your knitted panel is necessary and requires a careful series of steps to avoid confusion. These steps are a part of the technique that is laid out below. (At more advanced levels, you will be making separate, specially-edged panels and joining them, as you knit, to give you unlimited design capability.)

Here is stitch story for patterned whip-stitching:

The Gnomes' Adventure

Queen Lalalia got the word
From a far-flown message bird
That her cousin, Princess Nai,
Owned a carpet that could fly.

She summoned Knorg, her ablest Gnome,
Who'd been relaxing snug at home;
"Make me a carpet just like hers
And anything you want is yours!"

Knorg picked four gnomes, they went to see
The Wizard of the Hollow Tree;
"First, get yarn of mountain wool,
Night-spun when the moon is full."

"Then prepare the ties and loops,
Which we match and save in groups;
Next we make a special ring,
And tie a handy tugger-thing."

The Wizard said, "There's one more thing
From down the river you must bring:
The shed-skin of a flying snake;
We'll then your magic carpet make."

The gnomes went out and got a boat
And down the river they did float;
The fishes, as they bobbed along
Slapped their tails and sang a song.

The fishes led them to a nest
Where Iki coiled up at rest.
With amber beads and lumps of tin,
Knorg bartered for her molted skin.

Back upstream they paddled fast,
And reached the Wizard's house at last.
They stretched the skin and counted scales,
And marked them off with yarn tell-tails

One edge yellow, the other blue,
They wove them out all neat and true;
Then bent the snakeskin out and in,
And tied-off each tie to its twin.

Then at the bottom edge they hitched
An endless loop with which they stitched
And when the stitching-loop was gone,
Another loop was fastened on.

When the stitching was complete,
They worked the fabric, made it neat;
Tied-off the last stitch, pulled the ties,
Gave their thanks, said their goodbyes.

The gnomes then on the carpet sat,
Cried "Tandu!" and just like that,
The carpet flew them through the air
And landed in the palace square.

Queen Lalalia, with laughing eyes,
Granted Knorg his chosen prize:
A wild land of tangled trees,
Where gnomes still raise their families.

– H. Akin

Materials

For whip-stitching: 1 ball of Bulky wool yarn.
For stitching loops: 18 personal yards of Bulky yarn of a contrasting color.
For tell-tail ties:
Three yards of blue yarn,
Three yards of yellow yarn,
Three yards of red yarn.
For the ring loop: 8 inches of Bulky yarn in any color.

Preparation of Ties and Loops

For whip-stitching projects you will need several types of ties and loops: tell-tails, stitching loops, a tugger-loop and a ring-loop. (See key at the beginning of the chapter.)

Ties

For all projects in this chapter—practice to polished project—you will need a collection of color-coded tell-tail ties. It is convenient to prepare them all at once, even though not all of the ties will be used for every project. You will find it handy to keep them in a little pouch. Here, they will usually be referred to as "ties," as in "blue ties" and "yellow ties." These ties are each simply an 8-inch length of yarn to be folded in the middle and looped-on, either as flags to mark a spot in the work (tell-tails), or as basting-ties, to pin two selvedges together until they have been secured with whip-stitching.

Simply cut the yarn into 8-inch lengths. They will stand out better if the particular shades are at variance with the yarns you usually use. Ties are always removed from the work on completion, and should be set aside and re-used.

Preparing ties in these colors makes the communication of instructions clear and consistent, and this system will be used throughout.

For the projects in this chapter, you will need a little collection of ties in three colors. Prepare 10 blue, 10 yellow, and 4 red.

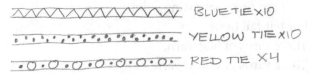

What Are Stitching-Loops?

Regular whip-stitching, like most kinds of hand-sewing, requires you to pull a strand through your work creating a seam. As the thread is used up and grows short, it is tied-off and the needle is re-threaded to begin another length. This is not much of a problem with thread, since the fine ends are easily tied-off and not so noticeable. But it would be unsightly to have a lot of yarn-ends in many of our barehand projects. Our solution is to use stitching-loops.

Stitching-loops are lengths of yarn that have been doubled over and felt-spliced together at the ends to form a loop of a personal-yard's length. This becomes a double-strand of yarn to stitch with.

The stitching-loop is Bare Hand Knitting's solution to the problem of having to draw a long length of yarn through the whole distance of a seam. While that was not a great inconvenience for the smaller projects shown earlier in this chapter, for larger projects it could become tedious. When the stitching-loop is about to run out, another loop is attached to it in the same way you join two rubber bands together. In this way we can make a series of smooth connections that magically blend into the knitting, with no knots and no ends!

For the stitching loops, select yarn that is the same thickness and type as your panel, but of a different color; one that contrasts in a pleasing way. The whip-stitches are both functional and decorative. (It is also actually much easier to work with contrasting colors.)

The number of loops you create will depend on the size of your project. For our practice project,

make 5 of them. If you end up with any extra loops, just keep them in your tell-tail pouch for later use.

Making Stitching Loops

Measure-off a personal-yard's length, double it over, and felt-splice the ends together.

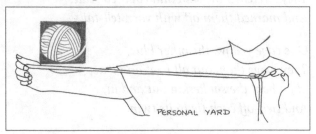

Avoid placing the felt splice at either end of a stretched-out loop, where tension will be greatest.

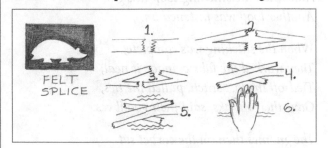

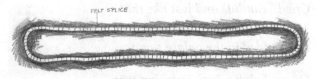

Once all of your loops are ready, smooth the strands together into lengths of doubled yarn. Once you have the 9 loops needed for the practice project, set them aside.

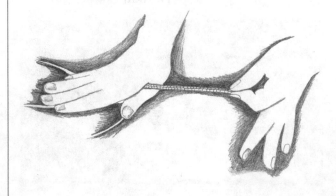

Tugger-Loop

While you are felt-splicing, you should also make a little tugger-loop that will be used along with the stitching-loops. Measure and cut a personal foot's length of yarn.

Loop it around and felt-splice the ends. Measure your tugger-loop by placing it next to your hand.

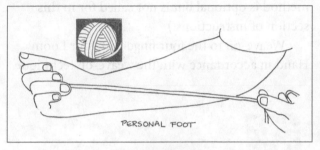

PERSONAL FOOT

Place your tugger-loop with your stitching loops and ties.

Ring-Charm

Using a ring-charm is optional. You will find that it almost magically helps the flow of your work by keeping the leed out of the way, and giving it just the right tension.

It is made in the same way as a tugger-loop, only a bit smaller—flattened, the loop is about the length of your ring finger. Set it aside with your other loops.

To employ your ring-charm, drape it onto Shuttle Ringa, give it a twist, lay the leed across the X of the twist, then slip the bottom loop over Ringa, snugging it down into a double-ring, holding the leed loosely in place.

Give the loop a twist.

Place the leed over the X formed by the twist.

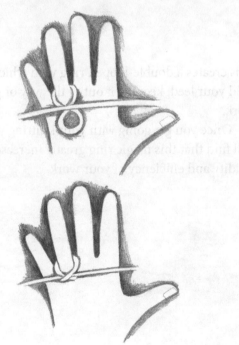

125

Place the top loop of your ring loop on the same finger.

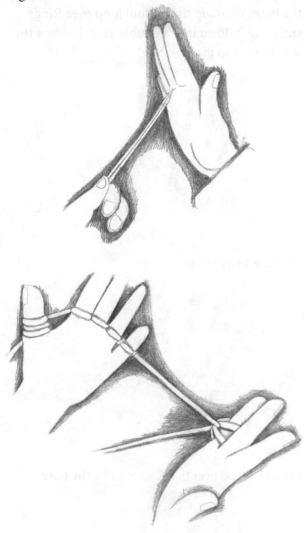

This creates a double-looped ring with which to hold your leed, keeping it out of the way of your work.

Once you get going with your knitting you will find that this magic ring greatly increases the fluidity and efficiency of your work.

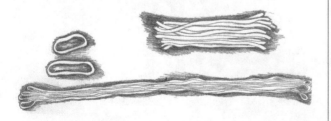

Create a Gnome Blanket

Knitting the Panel and Flagging Sections

When you are ready to start knitting, take up your ball of yarn and have five blue ties and five yellow ties ready within easy reach.

Knit a panel on one hand, marking sections of the column as you go. (Applying the frog-stitch method is optional but is not called for in this section of instructions.)

Weave-on to the four fingers of your Loom Hand in accordance with the weave-on technique.

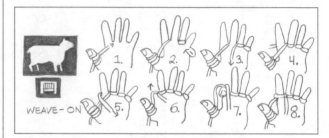

Knit an outbound-row, ending on Loom Pinky; but pause before knitting your return row.

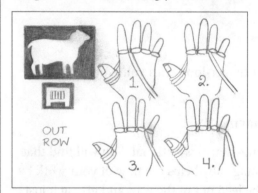

De-slack your weave-on, which will make for a snugger edge on your final piece.

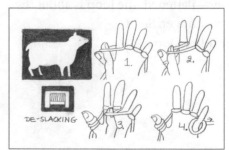

Lay the leed Thumbwise, and complete your first return-row.

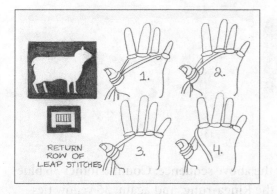

Keep knitting until you have at least 36 rows (18 out-and-return rows).

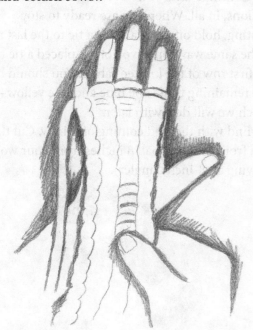

Counting Single Rows

Count out the rows by counting a column of moon stitches, or rungs, inward of the selvedge. The weave-on row counts for zero.

When counting out rows, it is helpful to use your Shuttle Thumb, inching it up each rung, as a place-marker.

Do not stretch out your knitted fabric by pulling on it at this time, as stretching the work will make the next step trickier to accomplish. (Specific instructions for stretching your work are included in a later phase of this project.)

Once you have counted up to the 36th row, take up a blue tie and attach it to Ringa's column. This is the long column of rungs that were knitted on your ring finger.

To do this, fold the tie in half, and secure it to the rung with a lark's head knot.

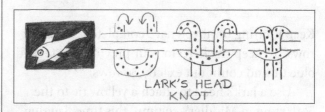

Gently tug on the ends, drawing the knot snug.

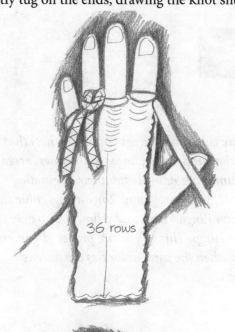

✳ You have flagged a section of knitting on a designated rung using a tie of a designated color.

127

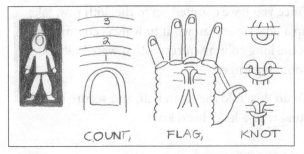

Keep knitting until you have completed 36 more rows. To keep track, go to your previously attached blue tie and count out exactly 36 rows.

Use a lark's head to attach a yellow tie to the 36th rung in Middler's column, this time flagging the end of your second section.

LARK'S HEAD KNOT

There are columns of rungs (ripple stitches) that accumulate under each finger as the rows increase. The columns are named after their originating fingers: Middler-rungs and Ringa-rungs. Blue ties go only on Ringa-rungs and yellow ties go only on Middler-rungs. This will assure proper alignment later on when the same-color ties are fastened together.

YELLOW TIE ON MIDDLER

36 rows

1st BLUE TIE ON RINGA

✳ You are now knitting, counting, and flagging sections of knitted fabric.

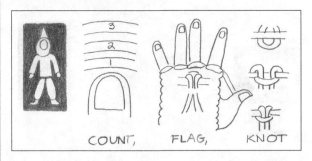

Repeat the above sequence: Count another 36 blue ties on the Ringa-rung, and again, 36 yellow ties on the Middler-rung.

Continue until you have nine delineated sections, in all. When you are ready to stop knitting, hold off on attaching a tie to the last row, in the same way you have not yet placed a tie on the first row of the knitted fabric. You should have two remaining ties—one blue and one yellow—which we will deal with later.

End with the leed coming off Pinky. Cut the leed from the yarn-ball 8 inches from your work (leaving an 8-inch dangler).

Secure-off your last row. Remember to tuck the loose end back into the ball.

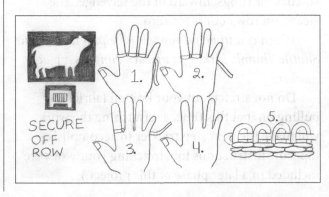

SECURE OFF ROW

1. 2. 3. 4. 5.

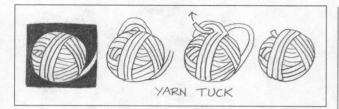

YARN TUCK

Weave-in the dangler just under the secure-off row.

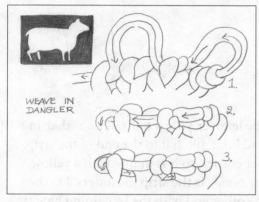

WEAVE IN DANGLER

1.

2.

3.

You may want to double check to make sure that the tell-tails are evenly spaced, making any necessary adjustments.

Laying Out the Knitted Fabric for Stitching

Lay the work out before you horizontally as best you can—you may have to bend the ends down to fit your working space. The cornfield stitches should be down. This means that the natural curl of the strip is upward, creating a channel all along the center-top of the strip.

The process of setting up the work involves several steps: condition the selvedges, weave-out the ties, place the knitted fabric into a meander, add the two end ties, and fasten matching ties, as described below.

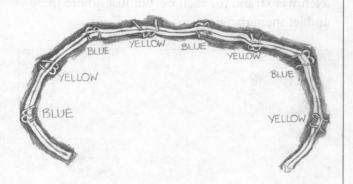

BLUE YELLOW BLUE YELLOW

YELLOW BLUE

BLUE YELLOW

Condition the Selvedge

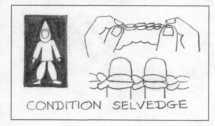

CONDITION SELVEDGE

Weave-Out Ties

Starting at the first blue tie, take the pair of tail strands and poke them down, just behind the nearest fishtail along the selvedge. Now, extend the two arms of each tell-tail for "weaving outward." Take up one end of the tie and poke it back up, through fish-lips—not the closest set of fish-lips, but the next fish-lips over. Take the other arm of the tie and, just as with the first arm (but going the opposite way), poke this one down behind the nearest fishtail, and, again, poke it back up through the 2nd pair of fish-lips over.

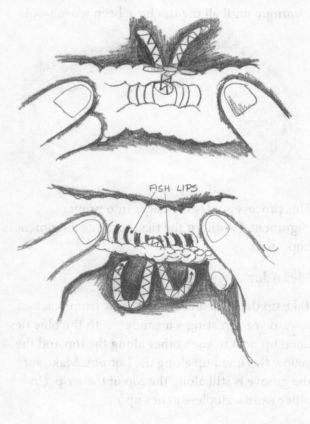

FISH LIPS

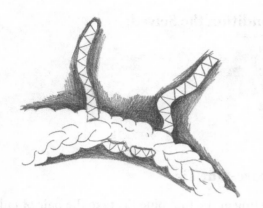

* You have now woven-out your first tie.

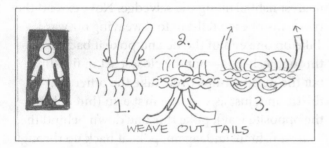

WEAVE OUT TAILS

Proceed to the next tie (yellow) and do the same. Continue until all the ties have been woven-out.

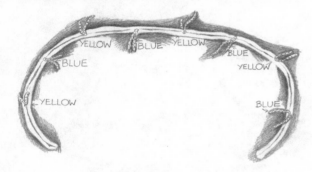

YELLOW   BLUE   YELLOW   BLUE

BLUE   YELLOW

YELLOW   BLUE

This process guides the edges into proper alignment. (Without the ties, accurate alignment is hopeless!)

Meander

Take up the strip and bend it away from you and toward you, creating a meander, with the blue ties lined up next to each other along the top and the yellow ties lined up along the bottom. Make sure the groove is still along the top of the strip. (In other words, ripple-stitches up.)

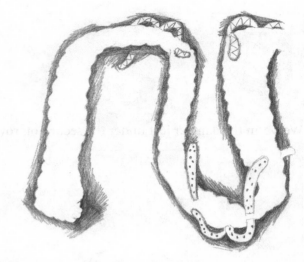

Take up the leftover yellow tell-tail tie and, using a lark's head knot, hitch it to the end of the strip, in the inner corner, so it is in line with a yellow tie near the bend, as the strip meanders. Do the same at the other end with the remaining blue tie, hitching it on the inner corner in line with a blue tie at the bend.

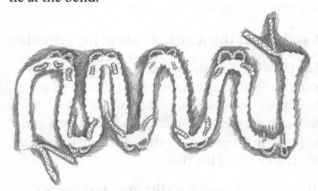

Using ties as fasteners, tie fairly loose square knots—that can be easily untied when needed—joining ties of the same color that are nearest each other. At the ends and outside bends you will have a leftover strand for each tie, but just ignore these and let them dangle.

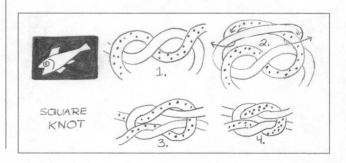

SQUARE KNOT

You have now loosely-attached the edges in proper alignment, and are ready to whip-stitch them together.

Now that you have knitted your panel, attached ties, woven-outward each tie, laid out the panel snake-style, added the two end ties, fastened the corresponding ties together, and checked your work to make any corrections; your piece is set-up and you can begin stitching.

Whip-Stitch Seams & Bridge Gaps

Pick up your tugger-loop and choose a stitching loop. Attach the tugger-loop to one end of the stitching-loop with a lark's head knot.

LARK'S HEAD KNOT

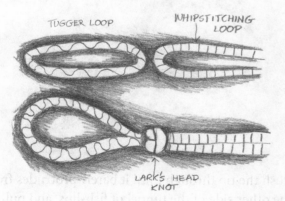

TUGGER LOOP

WHIPSTITCHING LOOP

LARK'S HEAD KNOT

Tie an overhand knot near one end. Smooth the strands together and tie the knot around your loom Pointer. Slip out your finger and snug-up the tug-knot. The little loop at the end should be about the size of the tip of your Pointer. You may place it closer to the tip or leave a small loop at the tip for tugging-on.

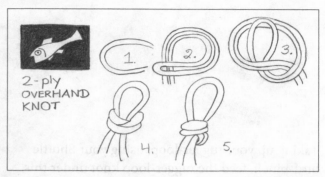

2-ply OVERHAND KNOT

1.
2.
3.
4.
5.

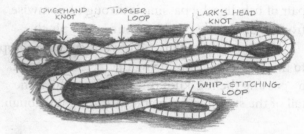

OVERHAND KNOT

TUGGER LOOP

LARK'S HEAD KNOT

WHIP-STITCHING LOOP

The tugger-loop is like a locomotive that hitches on to the front of your train of stitching loops and pulls them along, as a needle pulls thread.

First identify the fish-lips that are one section-in from the corner, and woven-through by the second-yellow-tie-in from the Loom side of the set-up piece.

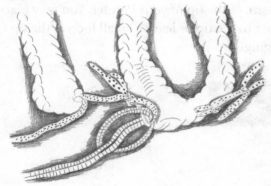

Taking up your tugger-loop, using your Shuttle bird-pinch, feed the tugger-loop knot under this pair of fish-lips, by passing it through Loomwise from your Shuttle pinch to your Loom pinch.

Now secure the tail-end of your stitching-loop to this pair of fish-lips using the lark's head knot, by passing the tug-knot through the bight at the tail of the stitching-loop and threading it through.

Begin the seam with a special stitch as follows:
Identify the corresponding pairs of fish-lips and get ready to feed the yarn through.

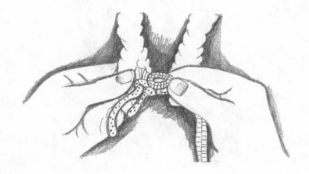

Push your Loom Thumb under and through both pairs of fish-lips, Shuttlewise, to open up a passage for the tugger-loop.

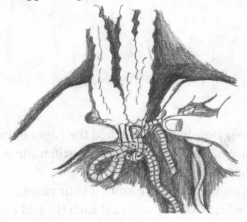

With your Shuttle bird-pinch, feed the tip back under both pairs of fish-lips, moving in a Loomwise direction, pushing your Shuttle Thumb against your retracting Loom Thumb to do so.

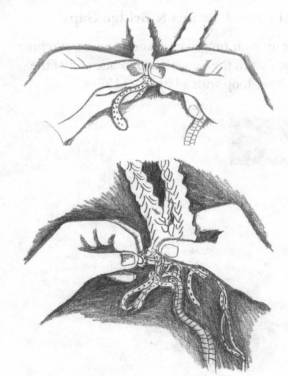

Push the tip through until it barely protrudes from the other side of the tunnel of fish-lips, and pull the entire yard's-length of two-ply yarn through.

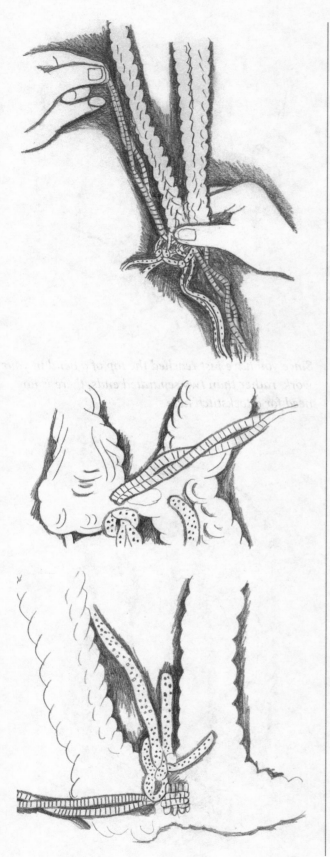

Insert the tug-knot back through the same hole a second time to secure the joining of two sections of knitted fabric.

❋ You have completed your first lockstitch.

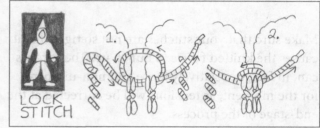

Go to the next set of corresponding fish-lips upwards of those you just stitched through, and work regular whip-stitches up the seam.

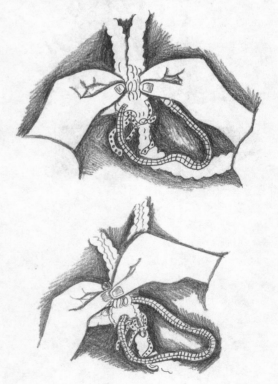

Continue to work your way up the seam of your piece, whip-stitching pairs of fish-lips and skipping fishtails. Stitch up the seam until you have reached the top corner of your columns and there are no pairs of fish-lips left to be matched.

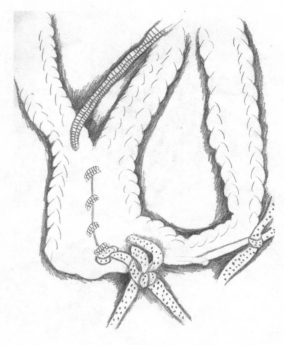

Make sure that your stitches are not so tight that it causes the knitted fabric to bunch up. The stitches can, in fact, be relatively loose and non-uniform for the moment, as tensions will be corrected at the end-stage of the process.

Since you have just reached the top of a bend in your work, rather than two separated ends, there is no need for a lockstitch here.

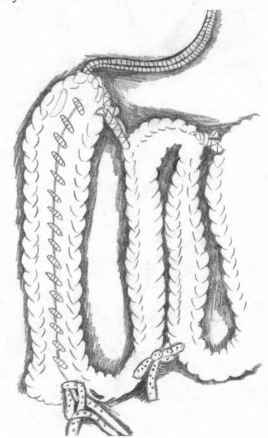

Rethreading the Loops for Stitching

Whenever your stitching-loop is running short, rethread the tugger loop.

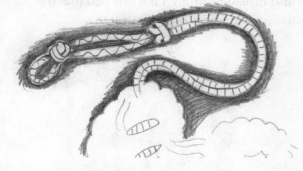

Loosen the lark's head knot connecting the tugger-loop and remove the tugger-loop.

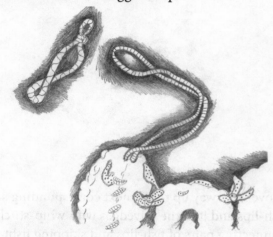

Attach the fresh stitching-loop to the shortened one with a lark's head, and re-attach the tugger; then continue stitching as before.

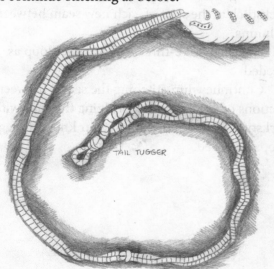

✴ You have just re-threaded your tugger-loop.

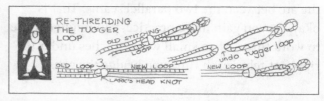

The meander of knitted fabric has a series of rounded arches along two sides. To allow for this, a group of five rows are left free of the stitchery at each curve. The ties were woven outward to accommodate this bend, and they now mark the proper placement for your next stitch. The start- and end-rows are the only exception to this rule, as you do not want your corners left sticking out in an unsightly manner.

Since you are again connecting two separated ends of the panel, a lockstitch is again called for, just as it was for your initial stitch.

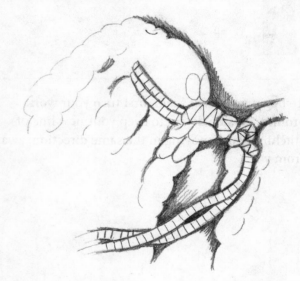

A several-inch stretch of yarn will remain, crossing the arc between the two parallel seams. That is okay. As you gain more practice, you might choose to work three-or-so small whip-stitches under the ripple-stitches each time you bridge the gap.

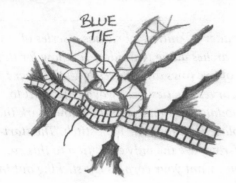

✻ You have now bridged a gap between meandered sections of knitted fabric.

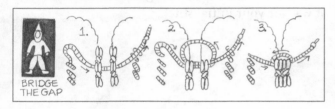

To begin your next seam, first turn your work around, topside down, to keep your new line of stitching-work moving in the same direction: away from you.

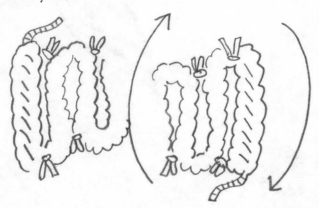

Thread the tug-knot down under the pair of fish-lips that the blue tie is drawn though, and bring the tug-knot across the gap to the next panel to also thread it through the fish-lips that the adjoining blue tie is drawn through.

Move your way up to the next corresponding set of fish-lips and join the selvedges with whip-stitches, connecting pairs of fish-lips and skipping fishtails, until you have reached the corner between sections, completing the stitching of another seam.

Bridge another gap, remembering to place a lockstitch at the start of each new seam between columns.

Continue to re-thread your tugger loop as needed.

Continue whip-stitching the seams between sections of knitted fabric, bridging the gaps with lockstitches, and rethreading your knotted tugger-loop as needed.

When you have worked your way down to the last set of fastened ties, hold off on stitching the last double-whip-stitch at the end until you have completed the following step for uniformity of stitches.

De-Slacking and Evening Tensions

De-slack your whip-stitches, simultaneously evening the tensions of the seams. Go back to the initial double-whip-stitch, at the starting-row and draw up slack one last time—this time making sure to leave even tensions in each stitch.

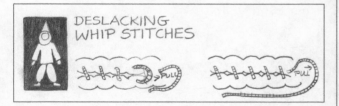

Once you have made all of your stitches relatively uniform, do an extra whip-stitch to bring the inner corner end-row in against the work.

Remove the tugger and snip the yarn-loop leaving about 8 inches extending. Then weave back up through the whip-stitched seam and, on the ripple side, tie the two ends off on each other near the middle of the piece.

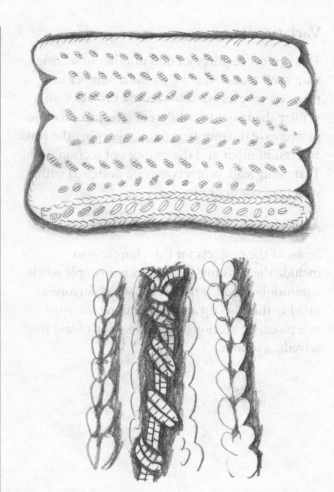

Remove the tell-tail ties and flip your work over.

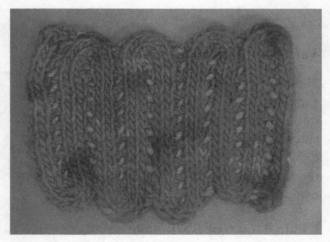

Variations

This project requires an odd number of sections, with each section having an even number of rows. If you ever want to create a project with a similar shape but in a different size, just increase or decrease the number of rows, keeping the rows an even number and the number of sections, odd. That being said, projects may be designed with a variety of configurations.

Additional Stitches

Some of the projects for this chapter also include the running stitch, another simple stitch commonly used for hemming, which involves moving the yarn up and down along the edge of a piece, for sections where you don't want the selvedges to join.

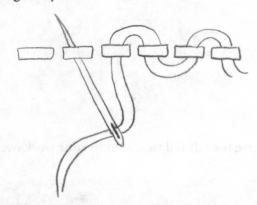

Variations of Stitching-Yarn

There are a variety of ways to configure stitching-yarn for your projects. You have already been introduced to the yarn-flow method and the stitching-loop method. The third way uses a different trick for temporarily shrinking down the length of your stitching-yarn: the chain-down method.

Chain-Down or Shrinkage

Use a stitching-yarn that is tightly spun or slick enough that it will not easily become snagged upon itself. Yarns made from plant fibers, such as cotton or flax, work best, but some wool yarns

have been used with success. Measure out the needed length for your project. Chain-knit all but a yard of it and place a tell-tail into the last loop of the chain.

Secure the unchained end to the fabric where you will be sewing.

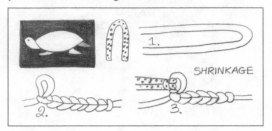

Yarn-snagging is more of a concern for teachers with a classroom of children, since each may require one-on-one assistance to continue.

If the yarn does snag on itself, gently remove the hindering fibers and proceed. Once yarn has been chained-down, you may tie a knot in the tip of the working end, or, if your thread is quite thin, tie it to the base of a knot tied in a thicker yarn for a good-sized tugger-knot.

Chapter Review for Whip-Stitching

Vocabulary Review

  seam
  tug-knot
  tell-tail
  stitching-loop
  tugger-loop
  fish-lips and fishtails
  meander
  lockstitch
  whip-stitch
  lark's head knot
  increase

Operations

Split and Fasten

Split yarn end.
Push one side of the split under the nearest rung.
Tie the two ends of the split off on each other.

Condition Selvedge

Stretch the selvedge to separate fishtails from fish-lips.

Attach Fringe

Prepare 14-inch strips of yarn.
Smooth strands into pairs.
Condition hole along edge of knitted fabric.
Fold pair of strands in half, making sure that ends match.
Push bight of fold up into hole, forming a loop.
Feed strands through hole creating a 2-ply lark's head knot.
Tug until snug.

Weave-Out Ties

Push tell-tails out under nearest fishtail. Bring one end back under a neighboring pair of fish-lips, Shuttlewise.
Bring the other end back under a neighboring pair of fish-lips, Shuttlewise.

Knit and Flag

Knit a given number of rows.
Count rows by rungs.
Attach tell-tail to a digital rung with a lark's head knot to flag a section.
Repeat until the desired number of sections have been knitted.
Re-thread your tugger-loop.

Lay Out Work

Check sections for accurate flagging.
Correct any mistakes.
Condition selvedge.
Weave-out tell-tails.
Bend knitted fabric into a meander.
Attach end-ties.
Fasten ties at corners.

Whip-Stitch Seams of Meanders

Stitch corresponding fish-lips, skipping fishtails, along selvedge.

Bridging

Draw stitching-yarn through fish-lips with ties.
Do a lockstitch.

De-Slack Stitching, Even Tensions

Pluck up the second stitch and gently tighten.
Pluck up each consecutive stitch, to de-slack, evening tensions as you go.
Pull extra slack into dangler before cutting and tying-off.

Projects for Whip-Stitching

Small-Sized Gnome's Vest

Materials

- 95 yards (roughly ½ of a skein of Bulky wool yarn
- 15 yards of stitching yarn in a contrasting color
- 8 blue tell-tail ties
- 8 yellow tell-tail ties
- 4 red tell-tail ties

A larger variation of this project makes a vest for a medium-sized sized gnome or doll vest.

Materials for medium-sized stuffed gnome or doll:

- 120 yards of Bulky wool yarn
- 20 yards of stitching yarn in a contrasting color.
- 8 blue tell-tail ties
- 8 yellow tell-tail ties
- 4 red tell-tail ties

Steps

Prepare panel

Frog weave-on:
1. Weave-on.
2. Complete initial outbound row.
3. Attach tell-tail to leed, next to Loom Pinky.
4. Complete initial return row.

Knit and flag panel:
5. Knit section of 18 rows and flag the 18th row with a yellow tie on Middler's rung and a red tie on Pinky's rung.
6. Knit a second section of 18 rows and flag the 9th row of the section with a red tie on Pinky's rung and the 18th row of the section with a blue tie in Ringa's rung. (The section size for a larger gnome vest is 24 rows.)
7. Knit 6 more sections of the same number of rows, alternating yellow ties on Middler's rung and blue ties on Ringa's rung.

The red ties will not be used again until the 8th section, where you will attach a red tie to the 9th row of the section on Pinky's rung and again in the 9th section where you will attach a red tie to Pinky's rung on the 1st row of the section.

Frog secure-off :
8. Frog-stitch, secure-off edge. and tie-off.
9. Frog-stitch, weave-on edge, and tie-off

Condition selvedge and set-op the piece:
10. Stretch out edges of knitted panel.
11. Weave-out the blue ties and yellow ties, but DO NOT weave-out the red ties.
12. Lay out knitted panel in a meander, cornfield stitches uppermost.
13. Gather the long panel, slalom style; blue ties toward you and yellow ties away from you.
14. Go back and attach a blue tie to the inner corner of the start-row and the inner corner of the finish-row.
15. Fasten your ties, yellow-to-yellow and blue-to-blue, and finally, red-to-red.

Stitching your piece:

16. Place a tug-knot into your stitching yarn.
17. Do a lockstitch to connect the finish-end to its connected corner.
18. Stitch a seam of whip-stitching.
19. Bridge the gap.
20. Turn the work around
    Leave first armhole opening
21. Secure the second line of the seam with a lockstitch. Pause whip-stitching.
22. Do several running stitches along one side of the new seam from the first red tie, at the start of the second seam until you reach the second red tie, midway down the same seam.
23. Do another lockstitch at the second red tie.
24. Resume whip-stitching the remainder of the second line of seam together.
25. Continue whip-stitching seams and bridging gaps up to the third red tell-tail at the start of the fifth line of seam.
    Leave second armhole opening.
26. When you reach the third red tie at the start of the fifth line of seam, secure it with a lockstitch, and pause whip-stitching.

27. Do several running stitches along one side of the new seam from the first red tie at the start of the second seam until you reach the second red tie, midway down the same seam.
28. Do another lockstitch at the second red tie. Whip-stitch the remainder of the seam.
29. Bridge the next gap, turn the work and whip-stitch the last two seams in the same way.
30. De-slack your entire piece, stitch-by-stitch from start to finish, making sure your stitches are snug and uniform.
31. Place a lockstitch through the last pair of fish-lips.
32. Snip the dangler and the tail at 8 inches.
33. Weave-in the tail and split-and-fasten it.
34. Do the same for the dangler.
35. Gently stretch out your piece, evening the tensions.
36. Place it, field stitches up, to view the upper side.

Flower Gnome Scarf

Materials

- 95 yards of Bulky wool yarn in a color of your choosing
- 10 yards of Bulky wool yarn in a contrasting color
- 2 tell-tails in blue
- 2 tell-tails in yellow

Steps

Prepare panel

Frog weave-on:

1. Weave-on.
2. Complete initial outbound row.
3. Attach blue tell-tail to leed, next to Loom Pinky.
4. Complete initial return-row.

Knit and flag sections:

5. Knit a section of 55 regular rows and flag Pointer's rung with a yellow tie.
6. Knit a section of 7 more regular rows and flag Pointer's rung with the second blue tie.
7. Knit a section of 55 more regular rows and flag Pointer's rung with another blue tie.
8. Knit a section of 33 regular rows and flag Pointer's rung with a yellow tie.
   Note: The knitted panel should now have 150 regular rows (equal to 75 out-and-return rows).

Frog-stitch secure-off edge and weave-on edge

9. Secure-off Thumbwise, without tying-off.
10. Place work with field-stitches uppermost.
11. Frog-stitch finish-end, Shuttlewise.
12. Turn work around with start-end on top, and field-stitches uppermost.
13. Remove initial 3 weave-on loops.
14. Frog-stitch start-end, Shuttlewise.
15. Tie-off the last frog-stitch.
16. Cut the dangler at 8 inches and place an overhand knot into the dangler to mark the finish-row.

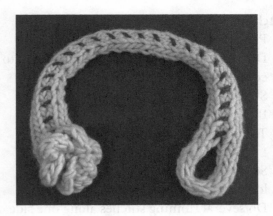

Stitch the piece

17. Lay the knitted panel out before you horizontally, ripple-stitches up, with the start-end to your Shuttle side and the finish-end to your Loom side, using the knot you placed on dangler to differentiate between the two sides, if necessary. (The dangler is always on the finish-end.)

Stitch the flower form

18. Place a tug-knot near the tip of your stitching thread.
19. Do 3 running stitches, working away from you, along, the frog-stitched edge of the finish-end (Loom-side) of the panel.
20. Now just lay your stitching-yarn Shuttlewise along the selvedge that is away from you, reaching the first blue tie.
21. You are now at the 8th row, the location of the blue tie. Work 3 running stitches back toward you.
22. Lay the stitching-yarn Shuttlewise along the selvedge nearest you, reaching the first yellow tie.
23. Work a third line of running stitches, moving away from you again.
24. Lay stitching-yarn Shuttlewise, along the selvedge away from you, reaching the next blue tie, which is the final tie.
25. Stitch back toward yourself again for a fourth and final line of running stitches.
26. Cut the stitching-yarn leaving 8 inches at either end.

27. Tug at both ends of the stitching-yarn, encouraging each fold to rotate into one petal of a 5-petal flower form, and tie-off the ends of the stitching yarn on each other.

28. Fold the remaining length of your knitted column—the part that does not make up the flower—in half at the midpoint, using square knots to attach blue-tie to blue-tie and yellow-tie to yellow-tie.

29. Tie a tug-knot into another length of stitching yarn.

30. Beginning at the seam between the blue ties, whip-stitch the parallel sets of fish-lips, joining the parallel selvedges into a seam until the yellow ties are reached, near the inner bend of your piece.

31. Snip the stitching-yarn leaving 8 inches at each end.

32. Weave-in the ends and split-and-fasten them to the work.

33. Push a length of dangler back under the last 3 whip-stitches on the ripple side of the scarf.

34. Weave-in the tail and split-and-fasten it. Do the same with the dangler.

35. Gently stretch out your piece, evening the tensions.

36. Place it, field-stitches up, to view the upper side.

Seat Cushion

Materials

- One skein of Bulky wool
- 6 stitching loops each of a personal-yard's length in yarn of a contrasting color
- 4 blue tell-tail ties and 4 yellow tell-tail ties
- Tugger-loop (optional)
- Yarn-ring (optional)

Steps

Prepare panel

Frog weave-on:

1. Weave-on.
2. Complete initial outbound row.
3. Attach tell-tail to leed, next to Loom Pinky.
4. Complete initial return-row.
5. Knit 36 regular rows of leapstiches.

Knit and flag sections:

6. Knit a section of 36 rows and flag Middler's rung with a yellow tie.
7. Knit a second section of 36 rows and flag Ringa's rung with a blue tie.
8. Repeat this action 5 more times, knitting sections that are each 36 rows long, alternating yellow ties on Middler's rung and blue ties on Ringa's rung until you have knitted a total of 7 sections in all.

Frog secure-off edge and weave-on edge:

9. Secure-off Thumbwise, without tying-off.
10. Place work with field-stitches uppermost.
11. Frog-stitch finish-end-edge, Shuttlewise.
12. Turn work around with start-end on top and with field-stitches uppermost.
13. Remove initial three weave-on loops.
14. Frog-stitch start-end edge, Shuttlewise.
15. Tie-off the last frog-stitch.
16. Cut the dangler at 8 inches and place an overhand knot into the dangler to mark the finish-row.

Condition selvedge and set-up the piece:

17. Stretch out edges of knitted panel.
18. Weave-out the blue ties and yellow ties.
19. Lay out knitted panel in a meander, cornfield stitches uppermost.
20. Gather the long panel into a meander, blue ties toward you and yellow ties away from you.
21. Go back and attach a blue tie to the inner corner of the start-row and the inner corner of the finish-row.
22. Fasten your ties, yellow-to-yellow and blue-to-blue.
23. Lay out the knitted panel in front of you, horizontally, cornfield stitches up.
24. Gather the long panel, slalom style, to obtain 12 meandering rows of equal length.
25. Fasten your ties to each other, yellow-to-yellow and blue-to-blue.

Stitching your piece:

26. Place a tug-knot into a stitching-loop (or attach knotted tugger-loop).
27. Attach stitching-loop to the inner corner of the first seam by pulling it through itself into a lark's head knot.
28. Stitch a seam of whip-stitch.
29. Bridge the gap and place a lockstitch at the start of the next seam.
30. Turn the work around.
31. Whip-stitch along the next seam.
32. Always attach new tugger-loops as needed. Repeat this pattern until you have stitched up the whole piece.
33. De-slack your entire piece, stitch-by-stitch from start to finish, making sure your stitches are snug and uniform.
34. Place a lockstitch through last pair of fish-lips.
35. Snip the dangler and the tail at 8 inches.
36. Weave-in the tail and split-and-fasten it.
37. Do the same for the dangler.
38. Gently stretch out your piece, evening the tensions.
39. Place it, field stitches up, to view the upper side.

Recorder Case

Prepare panel

Frog-stitch weave-on:

1. Weave on.
2. Complete initial outbound-row.
3. Attach tell-tail to leed, next to Loom Pinky.
4. Complete initial return row.

Knit and flag panel:

5. Knit a section of 151 rows.
6. Connect start-end and finish-end.
7. Flag third fish-lips over from connected seam.
8. Count 38 fish-lips from the first flag, topwise, and flag the next fishtail over at the midpoint.
9. Whip-stitch a seam from one flag to the next.
10. Cut the two ends of the stitching-yarn at 8 inches.
11. Weave the ends of the stitching yarn back under the seam of the work and split-and-fasten them.

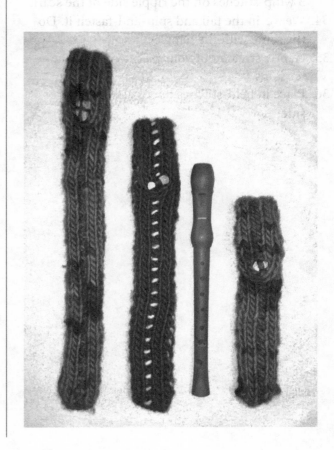

Create Your Own Designs

Be creative with your whip-stitching and come up with some fun designs of your own. I recently attended a workshop in Wilton, New Hampshire taught by Margaret Chambers who revealed the secrets of her unique gnome-making technique. She quoted an ancient gnome-knitter from Dornach, Switzerland, who confided, "If the gnomes are in your hands, you will make gnomes."

Let the wisdom in your hands lead you to the creation of barehand patterns of all types.

12. Fold the whole piece over, ripple stitches outermost, so that the side without the connecting-seam overlaps the side with the seam by about three fish-lips, creating a flap that will both close the case and hide the seam.

13. Beginning where the overlap begins, work whip-stitches down one side, connecting the doubled-over piece.

14. When the bottom of the seam is reached, weave the stitching yarn under the ripple stitches, bringing it to the base of the opposite seam.

15. Whip-stitch up the sides of the opposite seam.

16. Cut the stitching yarn at 8 inches on both sides.

17. Weave the ends of the stitching yarn back into their seams. Split-and-fasten their ends.

18. Finger-knit a short chain for a tie, or attach a shell with a hole, or other natural object to the outer case where the flap will cover, to serve as a button that the loose stitches can fasten around.

chapter eight

Wet-Felting

The Wonders of Wool

Barehand felting is a technique that can be combined with Bare Hand Knitting for more complex projects. I am including some basic projects to help you get your feet wet with this medium.

Felt is a wonderful matted fabric created primarily from wool. Wool, and to a lesser degree, fur, have a tendency to curl, interlace, and cling together when subjected to the influence of heat, moisture, and kneading or beating. The structure of woolen fiber is what gives it the ability to felt, or mat. The outer layer of wool hairs is composed of tiny scales. These scales are larger and more numerous than on human and most other hairs. The accompanying illustration of wool fibers as seen under magnification reveals the projecting edges of these scales, known as serrations.

The felting-value of wool is largely determined by the number of serrations per inch of fiber. These tiny scales hook on to each other when agitated. Also, since wool absorbs water, moisture—as well as alternating heat and cold together with movement and vibration—causes the tiny scales to lock more and more tightly onto each other. A small amount of plain mild soap added to the water has a relaxing effect on the scales of the wool so that the fibers slip in together more snugly. Other wooly fleeces, such as that of alpaca and angora, are similar and can be felted in the same way. Fibers such as camel hair, which have fewer scales, can be mixed with wool (at least 50/50 for best results).

Matted fabrics, such as tapa (Polynesian bark cloth) and felt, are thought to be the material used in the first clothing made by man, other than those made from animal skins.

You can find felt used in fashionable clothes of excellent quality, as well as durable and comfortable hats and shoes, or even in fabric art. The walls of Mongolian yurts are made of felt, and it is used for sleeping bags, furniture, insulation, fine soft jewelry, and countless other items.

In exploring this medium, and in consulting with a good number of felting teachers about projects for children and beginners, the surprising discovery is that each expert does it in a different way! There is more than one way to skin a catfish, as they say, and even more ways than that to form a felted ball; so don't be afraid to get your hands wet, and develop your own style. This book will tend toward the least complicated and most accessible and successful approaches. With practice you will find the balance that works best for you.

Story for Wet-Felting

Once, a mother turtle emerged from the waves and scooted up along a warm sandy beach to lay her eggs—on the same beach as used by her mother and grandmother before her. She carefully dug a deep round hole in the sand and laid a clutch of soft round white eggs into it.

She gently covered her eggs over and left them to the care of the sea and the sand. All through the long winter the tides ebbed and flowed, gently rocking

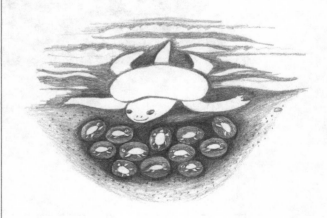

each round white eggs. So well-crafted was the hole that its roundness protected the eggs but never crushed them. With time, rocking movements, the foamy warm seawater and the rubbing of the sand against the eggshells toughened them, and the baby turtles inside were well protected from harm from any stray crab.

– A.B. Akin

Wet-Felting Station

Any wet-felting projects you take on will require you setting up a wet-felting station with the following items:

1. A container such as a small bucket that is wide open at the top, and at least 6 inches deep, filled with half a gallon of warm water.
2. An absorbent towel or other cloth.
3. Some water for a final rinse.
4. A teaspoon of vinegar (optional) to add to the final rinse.
5. About five tablespoons of pure soap; olive oil soap works well and is gentle on the hands.
6. Small dish (optional). If you are using bar soap you will want to soak it in a smaller dish of warm water to soften it.
7. A teaspoon of olive oil (optional) if you are not able to use olive oil soap or have sensitive skin.

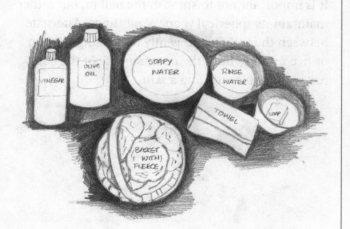

Wet-Felting a Ball

To make a ball, we will transform roving—wool that has been washed and combed, but not spun—into felt. This project can be done by people of all ages. Preschool and kindergarten-aged children love it. The balls make great toys—soft and safe for throwing about the house. Two variations follow: a set of 3 or 4 juggling balls.

For adults, a ball can be made in one sitting, in about three quarters of an hour. For young children it may be better to return to the project several times over the course of a few days. It is best to approach the activity as less product-oriented, and more process-oriented. And mainly, this project is a good jumping-off place for all the other felting projects encountered in this book.

Materials

You will need un-dyed wool roving in the amount of about 4 times the volume you want your ball to be—around 4 large handfuls (roughly 6 grams). Be sure it has not been super-washed.

If you wish your ball to have a colorful design, then a small amount of dyed wool roving is also needed.

Instructions

Take your measure of wool roving and gently pull it apart into thin strips about the size of turkey feathers. (Set aside any dyed roving for the last few layers of the ball.)

Before you begin wet felting, massage a bit of olive oil into your hands, giving it time to soak in. This will help to protect them from becoming irritated by the soap. Add the soap to the warm water, stirring it in well. You may want to keep a smaller dish with a more concentrated amount of soap handy, in case you need it.

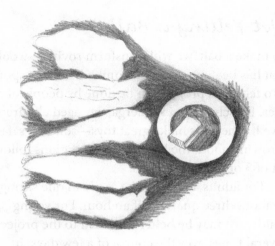

Form a Small Ball

Take one of your strips of roving and fold it over a few times at one end, then carefully pull and wrap the remainder of the strip around the fold, forming a little ball of sorts.

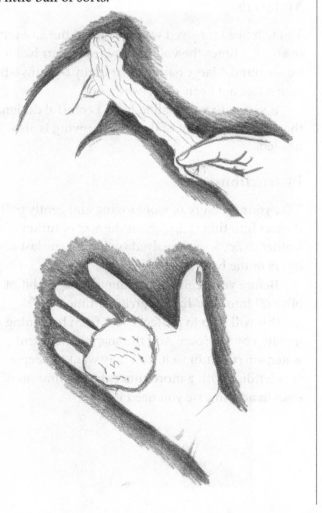

Dip-Drop-and-Roll

Dip the ball into the warm soapy water. Gently drop it back and forth between the palms of your hands. After dipping and dropping for a time, the fibers will begin to adhere to each other. At this point, cup the wet ball in your two hands and roll it gently between your palms. With enough soap you can also massage the surface of the ball.

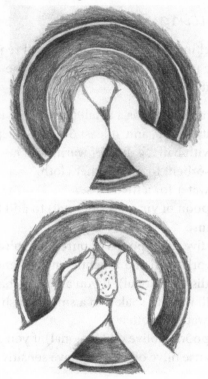

It is important not to smoosh the ball in, but rather maintain its spherical shape at all times. Alternate between the rolling and gently massaging for four or five minutes until the outer surface of the ball has sealed a bit, forming a *skin*.

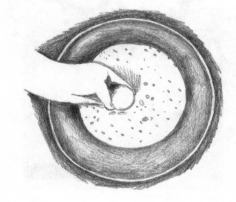

Adding Layers

You will proceed to *add another layer*, as follows:

Pick up another strip of roving and wrap it around your growing ball.

Dip the small ball in the water.

Continue to *dip-drop-and-roll* until a skin forms.

Take another length of roving and lay one end against the ball and secure it there with your Loom Thumb.

Gently pull the strip taut as you wrap it around the previous piece. Use the same approach as you would to roll a ball of yarn, shifting the angle of wrapping as you go to maintain the roundness of the growing shape.

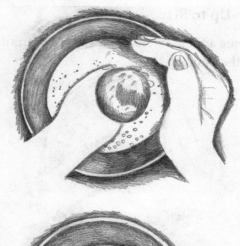

Dip the growing ball in water. Cup, roll, and gently massage the surface as before, until the surface forms a thin skin.

Dip the ball as needed. If the roving is sticking to your hands and not adhering to itself, just add more soap to your water or dip the ball into a more concentrated soap solution.

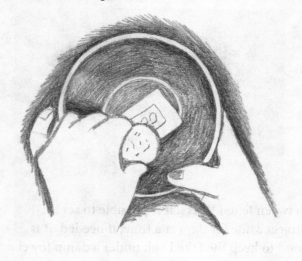

Layer-Up to Size

Continue adding layers in the same way until you reach the desired size.

Between felted layers, it is possible to set this project aside for days at a time, if needed. It is good to keep the felted ball under a damp towel between felting sessions. Always start with warm soapy water again for each new sitting.

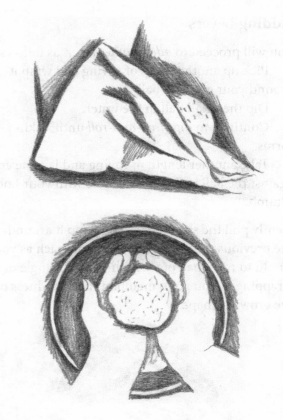

Rinse

When finished felting, empty your basin of warm soapy water and fill it with cool clean rinse-water. By adding a bit of vinegar to the final rinse, you will get out additional soap residue and further strengthen the surface. Dip your ball into the rinse water and gently squeeze out the soapy water. Repeat this several times until the water runs clean.

Let Dry

Leave your ball out to dry on a dry towel. It may take 24 hours to fully dry.

Add Color

To add dyed roving to decorate the surface of your ball you must tease out some very thin pieces of roving and apply them to the last layer or your ball before you dip it into the water. The texture of the dyed roving does not adhere as easily as un-dyed roving and you will want to gently rub it into the dry layer, using your fingertips to massage the edges together first.

Dip, cup, roll, and massage the surface as before. You will want to felt your last layer of wool for an especially long time to harden the outer skin. When you feel that the surface of your ball has integrity, you can stop.

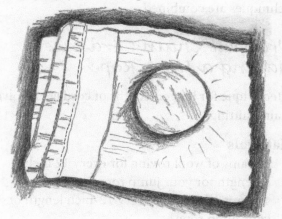

Felted Cordage

You can easily create lengths of felted cordage. For a practice swatch, make a simple felt tie. In the projects section you will need this technique to make the handles for a set of Poi Balls. In general, such soft yet strong cordage can be very useful for creating straps, structured hems, and countless other things.

Materials

- Wool roving in the amount of 6 large handsful, for every foot of cordage. Since you are making a single 12-inch length of cordage, you will need just that much.
- You will need to set up a complete wet-felting station as described for wet felting a ball.

Felting Screen

In addition, you will need a felting screen or mat that is about 18 inches wide, for rolling out the wet roving. A piece of burlap cloth works great. (Coffee roasters often have burlap sacks to sell cheaply or give away when asked.) The burlap works quite well although it will smell quite strongly of decaying plant materials when left wet for any length of time. For the most part, any variety of stiff woven fabric, soft screen, or thin matt will do the trick. Bamboo sushi mats are commonly used for a variety of wet felting projects. When you are a more advanced barehand practitioner, you will learn how to knit your own felt screen out of hemp yarn, but in the meantime, by all means experiment and find out what works for you.

Arrange Roving

Lay out on the burlap screen and take up a swath of wool roving to lay down on it. *Arrange the wool.*

Gently arrange the roving on the felting screen, pressing and tapping at it. Take up more of the fluffy, and slightly-sticky wool and continue to roll and press and shape it with your fingers, until you have a strip that is about 40 times thicker and 20% longer than you want the finished cord to be.

It is important and helps a lot for wet felting, in general, to have the wool more or less in place and somewhat consolidated in its form before wetting it.

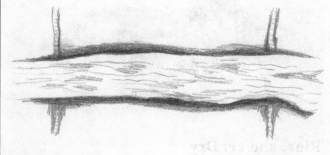

Roll Out

Fold the felting screen in half horizontally, closing it over the middle section of the wool and sprinkle water from your fingertips over the entire length of it.

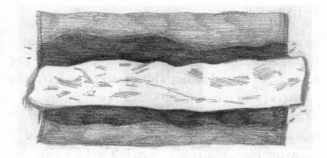

Gently roll out each of the sections: the middle and then the side sections of the wool, wetting it as needed, for several minutes for each roving.

Repeat this alternation, increasing the force and pressure of your rolling, until the cordage is felted, has formed a skin, and has integrity.

Rinse and Let Dry

Rinse-and-squeeze several times, in clean water. You may add a bit of vinegar to your rinse or alternate a cold with a hot rinse to further harden your piece to the desired toughness.

Variations

Once you are practiced at wet-felting cordage, you can try to layer-up cordage using changing colors of wool to make it thicker. You can slice it into ½-inch wide cylindrical pieces to be used as beads or for general decorative purposes in your designs. For best results, be sure that each layer is more-or-less felted before adding the next layer, and make certain that each new added layer of color wraps fully around the cylinder so it can adhere to itself. This technique works for shorter lengths of cordage. A technique for longer lengths also involves chain-knitting and is introduced at a more advanced level of Bare Hand Knitting when techniques are combined.

Wrapped-Chain Cordage: Making a Jump Rope

A technique for longer lengths of cordage involves chain knitting.

Materials

- 2 grams of wool roving for every 12 inches of length for your jump rope
- 4 grams of sand for every 12-inch length of your jump rope
- Wet felting station.

Instructions

Knit a length of chain of the desired length for your cordage.

Wrap thin strips of wool roving snugly around the chain.

Once the entire length of rope has been wrapped in a thin strip of wool roving, add a second layer. This time, however, sprinkle sand onto the strips of roving as you wind them on. This adds weight to the jump rope.

Build up about three layers of thickness and begin to wet felt. Gently roll the cordage, back and forth, section by section, with your bare hands.

Once it forms a skin, you can roll the whole length of it into a coil.

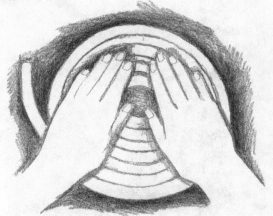

Repeat this process by flipping and rewinding it from different angles, as needed.

You can slip the cordage back and forth through your hand, squeezing it slightly, to further felt it.

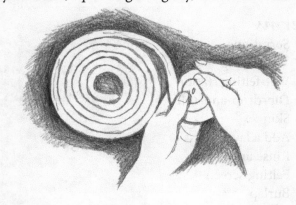

Once the whole rope is adequately felted, rinse out the soap, hang, and let dry. For a better grip, place an overhand knot near both ends of the rope.

OVERHAND KNOT

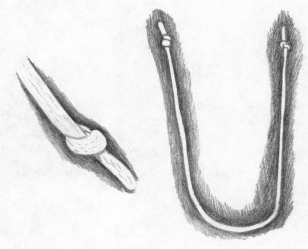

Vocabulary for "Wet-Felting"

Terms

Serrations
Wet-felting
Wet-felting station
Dip-drop-and-roll
Skin
Add a layer
Rinse and let dry
Felting screen
Burlap
Arrange the wool
Roll

Wet-Felting Projects

Circus Fun!

Utilizing the skills learned in this chapter, it is possible to make many things. Beginning here with juggling balls, poi balls, and jump ropes, you are well on your way to creating the equipment for your own circus act. Circus skills incorporate movements that cross both the vertical and horizontal midlines in the body and in the brain. Developing these skills (both for making them and for using them) is a wonderful way to develop the senses of balance and movement, and to stimulate the vestibular system in ways proven by research to be helpful in human development. Circus skills help you to have a good time while you're at it, too!

Catching up on Components

A note on crafting projects with sets of two or more of the same item: try to craft the entire set, simultaneously. In other words, whenever you come to a resting point, catch up the other matching items to the same point before moving forward. Suggestions for when to do this are placed into the steps in the form of a reminder to: *Catch up component pieces to this stage.*

Juggling Balls: Set of Three

Materials

Set up a wet-felting station, as described in this chapter.

You will need un-dyed roving in the amount of about four handsful for each ball: 12 large handsful of un-dyed roving, altogether.

You will also want a small amount of colored roving (about a half a handful per ball) in two or more different colors, one for each ball.

Find three small, roundish stones of equal size—about the size of a large grape—that will remain inside of your balls.

Steps

1. Separate your roving into strips.
2. Oil your hands.
3. Add soap to your warm water.
4. Form a little ball of roving around a stone.

5. Gently dip-drop-and-roll the little ball till it forms a skin.
Catch up component pieces to this stage.

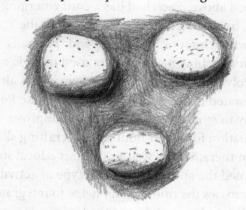

6. Build up another layer into a skin.
Catch up component pieces to this stage.

7. Continue building up layers in this way until the desired size is achieved.
Catch up component pieces to this stage.

8. Add color by wrapping several thin strips of colored roving around your complete-sized ball so that each strip overlaps itself at the ends. Adding multiple colors can also be interesting.
9. Dip-drop-and-roll the little ball of wool.
10. Build up another layer or two of color or colors until the surface of the ball is enveloped in colored roving.
Catch up component pieces to this stage.

11. Set out your three balls to dry on a cloth for about 24 hours.

A Pair of Poi Balls

Poi balls are about the size of the juggling-balls described above. Each ball has a cord emerging from it, between 2 and 3 feet long—to fit the user—with a knot or loop at the end. The balls come in matching pairs, and are used in Hula and other Polynesian dances, and are sometimes also incorporated into circus acts. The Maori use Poi ball play to strengthen the wrists and improve coordination for better hunting and crafting skills. Modern therapists, as well as Waldorf educators, have noted the advantages of this type of activity, which crosses the midline and helps to integrate left and right hemispheres of the brain.

Parts

Each poi ball is composed of a ball of felted wool roving, an inner "anchor stone," a braided cord of strong, non-stretchy material such as cotton, hemp or linen, and a looped felted-wool handle.

Materials

- *For balls:* You will need roughly 4 grams of undyed wool roving. (2 grams per ball). Optional: additional colored wool roving for a decorative outer layer.

- *For anchor stones:* Two flattish stones, roughly the size of large grapes.
- *For cords:* Six lengths of cotton, hemp or linen yarn, each 3 personal yards long. (Total: 18 yards.)
- *For handles:* 4 grams of wool roving; two 18-inch lengths of cotton, hemp or linen string for whipping handles onto cords. (Alternately, for chain-knitted handles, 6 yards Bulky wool yarn.)
- *To work:* A complete Wet-felting station as outlined in this chapter.

Shrinking the Strings

To make the six strings easier to work with, we will chain-knit about half the original length of each, giving us about 18 inches of chain on each. At that point, insert a tell-tail with a lark's head knot as a stopper. This is called *chaining-down*, or *shrinking*. Later, we will pull out the tell-tails and unravel these chains.

Make sure when you begin chain-knitting, that you start close enough to one end that the tail is no more than 6 inches long. This is so that you don't accidentally attach the wrong end to the stone, which would cause problems.

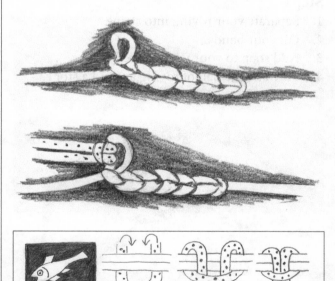

LARK'S HEAD
KNOT

Prepare the Stones

Now, tie three of the prepared strings to each stone. Attach the long end of each unchained portion of string, coming from the tell-tail. Fasten the three strings in any way that will hold while you work, since the felting process will make them secure. Each string should come away from the stone at a different point.

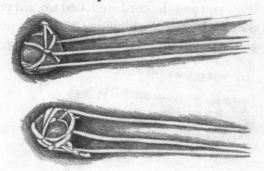

Shape the Balls

You will now be *wet-felting the balls* as described in this chapter, only here you will be working around and with the strings. To begin with, *shape a ball* by wrapping a small strip of roving carefully around a stone, arranging it in such a way that it lies between and around the three tied-on strings, separating them from one another.

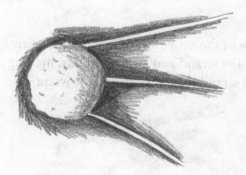

Dip-drop-and-roll till your little wool ball forms a skin.

Catch up component pieces to this stage.

Build up layers, arranging each new layer of wool in such a way so as to separate the three strings from each other. At this point, it is all right if the strings emerge in different directions.

Catch up component pieces to this stage.

Continue to build layers in the same way till the ball is roughly half the size it will be; the final size should be about the size of an orange.

Catch up component pieces to this stage.

Merging the Strings

Once the ball is built up to roughly half its size, it is time to *merge the strings*. You will want to gradually bring the three strings closer together. Always dip-drop-and-rolling until a skin begins to form on each layer before adding the next.

Finally, the three strings will emerge from the same point, at the surface of your ball, secured in place by the final layers of felt.

As an option, you may want to add a layer of colored felt to the outer surface.

Catch up component pieces to this stage.

Rinse the soap from the two poi balls with cool water and a dash of vinegar.

Braid Strings into Cords

Once each ball is completed, and even before they have dried, you can braid the strings as follows: beginning where they emerge from the ball, braid the three strings together. When the braid reaches your tell-tails, remove each tell-tail and unchain about half the chain on each string, then re-insert the tell-tail. Do this for each of the three strings on each ball.

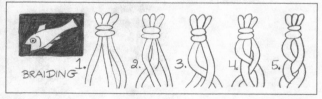

Resume braiding until you again reach the tell-tails. At this point, unravel the rest of the chains.

Now it is time to check your measurements and make adjustments, so that the cords are matched in length, and that the length is the right size for the intended user. This is done by folding the unbraided strings over to make loops, and loosely tying them off with overhand knots.

Catch up component pieces to this stage.

Check the length of each cord by measuring from the point where it emerges from the ball to the fold in the loop at the end. This distance should equal a personal yard. You can make adjustments by refastening each loop so that it is larger or smaller, until the desired size is reached. Make all three end-loops reach the same point, which is the key goal, rather than having the loops all the same size.

Smooth the loops flat and continue braiding them until there is only a small loop, about an inch long, at the end of each string.

Catch up component pieces to this stage.

Making Handles

Felted-Cordage Handles

Using your 4 grams of wool roving, follow the instructions earlier in this chapter to make two lengths of one-foot-long felted cordage.

In preparation for attaching the handles, lay out one of your felt balls before you with the ball away from you and the cord stretched toward you.

Take up a length of whipping string and run it through the double loops to the half-way point.

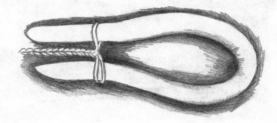

Wrap one end of the string tightly around the base of the handle, three times.

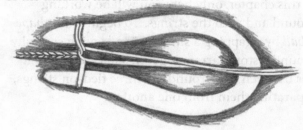

Half-twist the active strand around the resting side of the strand and switch strands, making the resting strand the active strand for wrapping.

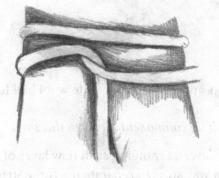

Continue wrapping toward the bight in the handle alternating in this way, until you have about an inch of whipping securing the handle to the cord.